Object-Oriented Technology:

A Manager's Guide

David A. Taylor, Ph.D.

ADDISON-WESLEY PUBLISHING COMPANY, INC.
Reading, Massachusetts   Menlo Park, California
New York   Don Mills, Canada
Wokingham, England   Amsterdam   Bonn
Paris   Milan   Madrid   Sydney   Singapore
Tokyo   Seoul   Taipei   Mexico City   San Juan

The publisher offers discounts on this book when ordered in
quantity for special sales. For more information please contact:

Corporate & Professional Publishing Group
Addison-Wesley Publishing Company
One Jacob Way
Reading, Massachusetts 01867

Many of the designations used by manufacturers and sellers
to distinguish their products are claimed as trademarks. When
those designations appear in this book and Addison-Wesley was
aware of a trademark claim, the designations have been printed
in initial caps.

The programs and applications presented in this book have been
included for their instructional value. They have been tested with
care, but are not guaranteed for any particular purpose. The publisher does not offer any warranties or representations, nor does it
accept any liabilities with respect to the programs or applications.

Cover Art: © 1981, Jay Dunitz, Kroeber Series #45
Book design by Abrams Design Group

ISBN 0-201-56358-4

4 5 6 7 8 9 10-DO-95949392
Fourth printing September 1992

Preface

Object-oriented technology is arguably the most exciting and least understood development in software today. Given the amount of hype coming from both media and manufacturers, it's hard for corporate managers to assess its true potential.

This problem is of great concern to us at Servio. We see object-oriented technology as an important step toward the industrialization of software, in which programming is transformed from an arcane craft to a systematic manufacturing process. But this transformation can't take place unless senior managers understand and support it.

What the industry needs right now is a straightforward explanation of object-oriented technology at the management level, with a candid assessment of its real costs and benefits. As one of the leading innovators in object-oriented technology, Servio is in a unique position to provide that explanation. We have devoted the resources to carry out this task as a service to the industry as a whole, not to promote our own products. We believe that everyone will be better served by a clearer understanding of the transition we are about to make.

What you have in your hand, then, is our contribution to executive education – a no-nonsense explanation of the concepts and issues involved in object-oriented technology. We hope that David's clear, readable discussion will counter some of the hype surrounding this new technology and help you make more informed decisions about adopting the technology within your own company.

Servio Corporation
1420 Harbor Bay Parkway
Alameda, CA 94501
(800) 243-9369

Acknowledgment

Servio Corporation thanks Dan Doernberg, CEO of Computer Literacy Bookshops, who was instrumental in bringing this book to the attention of Addison-Wesley. Computer Literacy's San Jose store was the first store to carry this book prior to its publication by Addison-Wesley.

Table of Contents

Introduction

This guide introduces a new approach to building software systems – object-oriented technology. The purpose of the guide is to help you make more informed decisions about adopting object-oriented technology within your company.

This guide introduces object-oriented technology

Unlike most books on the subject, this guide is written for managers, not engineers. I've kept the technical details to a minimum and introduced jargon only as necessary to explain the technology. I don't assume that you know how to program a computer or even use one, but I do assume that you are generally familiar with computers and how they are used in business.

It's written for managers

To help you in your evaluation, I've tried to go beyond the hype that surrounds object-oriented technology and take an honest look at its advantages and limitations. Moreover, the guide doesn't favor any particular product, language, or approach to defining object-oriented technology. What it favors is good management solutions.

It offers an objective appraisal

My main objective is to develop the business case for object-oriented solutions, not to explore the technology for its own sake. Inevitably, I've had to gloss over some difficult technical issues and present simplified versions of the essential concepts. The result is a practical, decision-making perspective rather than a more rigorous theoretical analysis.

The guide is business oriented

You can read this guide selectively

If your interest is in selecting the right tools and supervising an object-oriented project, you should read the guide straight through. If you prefer a high-level overview, read Chapters 1 and 2, which introduce the basic concepts, then skip to the end of the guide and read Chapters 7, 8, and 9, which show how these concepts are applied in practice. There is also a "fast track" on the outside of the page that you can use to get a running summary and read sections selectively.

There's also a glossary and summary of key concepts

The guide also contains a glossary and a summary of key concepts. The glossary defines all the terms that appear in **boldface type**. The summary of key concepts briefly outlines what I regard as the ten essential concepts of object-oriented technology.

1

Beating the Software Crisis

Modern corporations are faced with a profound dilemma. Increasingly, they are becoming information-based organizations, dependent on a continuous flow of data for virtually every aspect of their operations. Yet their ability to handle that data is breaking down because the volume of information is expanding faster than the capacity to process it. The result: corporations are drowning in their own data.

Corporations are drowning in data

The problem doesn't lie in hardware – computers continue to increase in speed and power at a phenomenal rate. The failure lies in software. Developing software to tap the potential of computers turns out to be a far greater challenge than building faster machines.

The failure lies in software

The Software Crisis

The gap between the potential of hardware and the performance of software is getting wider all the time. This wasted potential affects everyone who uses computers, but it places a special burden on large corporations, which depend heavily on their ability to construct dependable, large-scale information systems. It's now a rare development project that comes in anywhere near on time, much less under budget. Worse yet, the systems created by these efforts are typically riddled with defects, and they are so rigidly structured that it's nearly impossible to make major changes without totally redesigning them.

Most software is delivered late and over budget

Combine these problems with the increasing rate of change in business conditions today and you have a recipe for disaster. Most corporate software is obsolete long before it's ever delivered, and it is usually incapable of evolving to meet future needs. Studies of this problem indicate that in some cases as little as five percent of all software development projects result in working systems; the rest are sent back for reconstruction, abandoned after delivery, or never even completed.

We need better software and we need it faster

This situation is known in the industry as the **software crisis**. It is a problem of major proportions, and it threatens the viability of all modern information-based organizations. Resolving this crisis is rapidly becoming one of the prime concerns of corporations throughout the world.

How Software Is Constructed

Clearly something is wrong here. It's not that we haven't tried to improve our techniques for building software. Rather, it's taken us years to understand just how hard it *is* to build good software. Developing robust, large-scale software systems that can evolve to meet changing needs turns out to be one of the most demanding challenges in modern technology.

The remainder of this chapter summarizes what I regard as the major efforts to meet this challenge. By reviewing what's been tried before, I want to set the stage for understanding how the object-oriented approach is different from earlier methods, and why it should succeed where others have failed.

Building Programs

A program is nothing more than a series of instructions that tell a computer to carry out specific actions. Small programs can be built as a single **procedure**, or sequence of instructions, that performs the desired task. Single-procedure programs are usually written by a single programmer, who can maintain a mental image of the entire procedure, move instructions from place to place, and make design decisions freely as the program unfolds. Small groups of programmers can work in a similar style so long as all the members have free and open communication with each other.

Larger programs can't be constructed as a single procedure like this. As the size of a program grows, so does the number of programmers required to build it. When a development group numbers in the tens or hundreds, the amount of communication required among the programmers becomes overwhelming. So many people are negotiating so many interacting decisions that no one has time to do the actual programming!

Modular Programming

In principle, the solution to this problem is straightforward: break large-scale programs down into smaller components that can be constructed independently, then combine them to form the complete system. This general strategy is known as **modular programming**, and it forms the guiding principle behind most of the advances in software construction in the past forty years.

Larger systems require modular programming

The most elementary support for modular programming came with the invention of the **subroutine** in the early 1950s. A subroutine is created by pulling a sequence of instructions out of the main routine and giving it a separate name; once defined, the subroutine can be executed simply by including its name in the program wherever it is required. Subroutines provide a natural division of labor: different programmers write the various subroutines, then assemble the completed subroutines into a working program.

Subroutines support modular programming

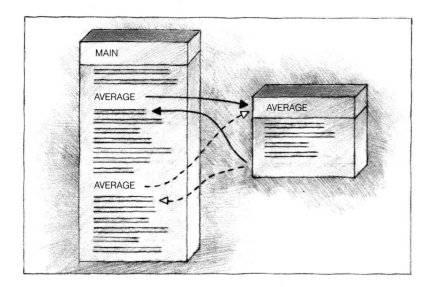

Subroutine called from two places

But modular programming requires discipline

While subroutines provide the basic mechanism for modular programming, a lot of discipline is necessary to create well-structured software. Without that discipline, it is all too easy to write tortuously complicated programs that are resistant to change, difficult to understand, and nearly impossible to maintain. And that's what happened far too often during the early years of the industry.

Structured Programming

Structured programming provides that discipline

In the late 1960s, the generally poor state of software sparked a concerted effort among computer scientists to develop a more disciplined, consistent style of programming. The result of that effort was the refinement of modular programming into the approach known as **structured programming**.

Functional decomposition plays a central role

Structured programming relies on **functional decomposition**, a top-down approach to program design in which a program is systematically broken down into components, each of which is decomposed into sub-components, and so on, down to the level of individual subroutines. Separate teams of programmers write the various components, which are later assembled into the complete program.

Program with 2 levels of nesting

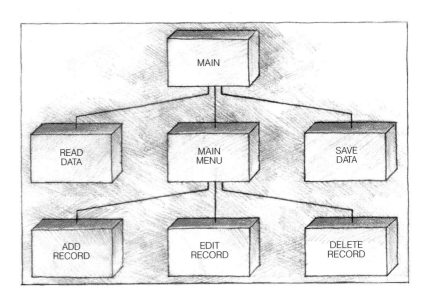

Structured programming has produced significant improvements in the quality of software over the last twenty years, but its limitations are now painfully apparent. One of the more serious problems is that it's rarely possible to anticipate the design of a completed system before it's actually implemented. Once the programming is underway, what seemed like a good division of labor at the outset turns out to be the wrong allocation of problems to modules, and the entire design has to be reworked from the top down. The larger the system, the more often this restructuring may take place.

Structured programming is useful but limited

Computer-Aided Software Engineering (CASE)

The latest innovation in structured programming is computer-aided software engineering (**CASE**). With CASE, computers manage the process of functional decomposition, graphically defining subroutines in nested diagrams and verifying that all interactions between subroutines follow a correctly specified form. Advanced CASE systems can actually build complete, working programs from these diagrams once all the design information has been entered.

CASE automates structured programming

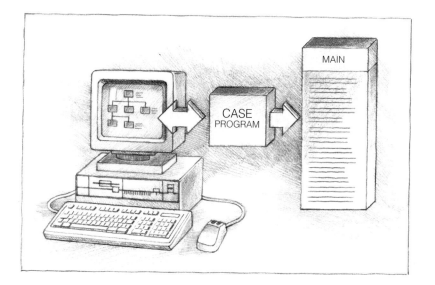

CASE building a program

Proponents of CASE herald the automatic generation of programs from designs as a major breakthrough in software development. However, the process is not nearly as automatic as it first appears. In fact, a CASE tool doesn't create software at all – it simply translates the design for a system from graphical to textual form. Experience to date has shown that developing a complete graphical design for a program can be just as demanding and time-consuming as writing the program in the first place.

Fourth-Generation Languages

Another approach to automatic programming is represented by **fourth-generation languages** (**4GLs**), so called to distinguish them from the conventional "third generation" languages discussed above. 4GLs include a wide range of tools to help automate the generation of routine business applications, including the creation of forms, reports, and menus.

4GLs offer many advantages, including the fact that people who are not programmers can use them. The down side of 4GLs is that they can only generate rather simple programs and then only for well-understood problems. Although a programmer can modify these programs by hand to make them more sophisticated, the 4GL can no longer be used to maintain the modified programs. Useful as they are, 4GLs are quickly left behind for all but the simplest applications.

Managing Information

Most efforts to improve software development have focused on the modularization of procedures. But there is another component to software which, while less obvious, is no less important. That is the data, the collection of information operated on by the procedures.

As the techniques of modular programming have evolved over the years, it has become apparent that data, too, must be modularized.

Data Within Programs

If a program requires only a few pieces of data to do its work, these pieces can safely be made available to all the different subroutines that make up the program. This arrangement is very convenient for programmers because the shared collection of data provides a communal "blackboard" on which the various subroutines can exchange information whenever they need to communicate.

Subroutines can share small amounts of data

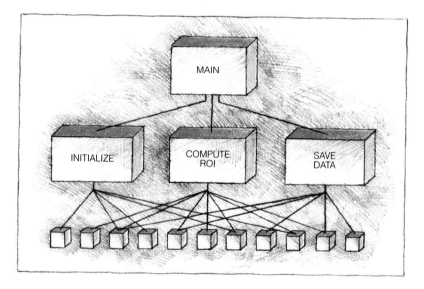

Shared data with multiple subroutines

When the pieces of data number in the hundreds or thousands, however, this simple solution usually leads to mysterious errors and unpredictable behavior. The problem is that sharing data is a violation of modular programming, which requires that modules be as independent as possible. Allowing modules to interact freely through shared data makes the actions of any one module directly dependent on the behavior of all the others. In effect, the shared pool of data becomes the chink in the armor that structured programming has built around the subroutine.

But sharing too much data leads to problems

The solution lies in hiding information

The solution to this problem is to modularize the data right along with the procedures. This is typically done by giving each subroutine its own local store of data which it alone can read and write. This strategy of **information hiding** minimizes unwanted interactions between subroutines and allows them to be designed and maintained more independently.

Local data within subroutines

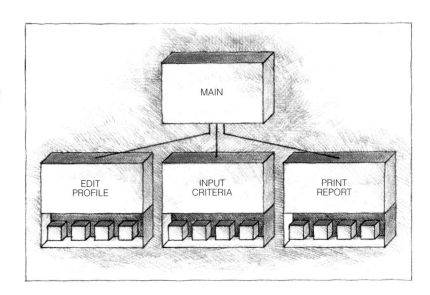

Data Outside of Programs

Some programs don't need to preserve data

Small programs often require only a few inputs and generate output that is meant to be consumed immediately. A program to calculate amortization tables, for example, might accept a base value and an amortization period from the keyboard, then print out a page of calculations. Programs of this sort don't need to store any data because they work with fresh information every time they are run.

But most large programs have to reuse data

Larger programs, however, usually work with the same information over and over again. Inventory control programs, accounting systems, and engineering design tools couldn't function if they didn't have a way of preserving information from one run to the next.

The simplest solution to the problem of keeping data around is to have a program store its data in an external file. When you finish running the program, it sends the data to the external file. When you start up the program again, it retrieves the data from the file. The use of a file also allows the program to work with more information than it could hold internally by reading and writing only a small portion of the file at any one time.

Data can easily be preserved in files

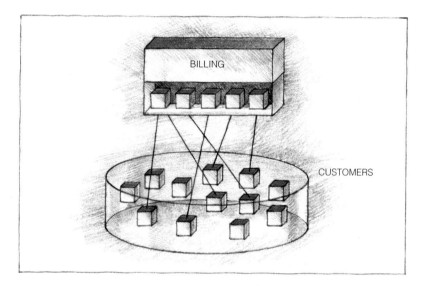

A program accessing a file

External data files provide an adequate solution for information storage so long as the data is accessed only by a single person using a single program. When data has to be shared, new problems arise.

But that doesn't work when data must be shared

Sharing Data

When different people can access the same file, there's always the possibility of one person changing information that others are currently using. Preventing this confusion turns out to be a fairly difficult technical problem that is not easily solved within a simple file system. Although some older programs still use files to store shared information, most multi-user systems are now built on top of special programs, called **database management systems (DBMSs)**, that are designed to manage simultaneous access to shared data.

Shared data requires a database management system

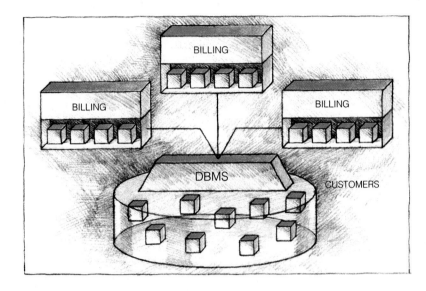

Databases contain structure as well as data

Database management programs do more than just control access to data stored in files; they also store relationships among the various data elements. The earliest form of database manager, known as the **hierarchic model**, represented data items (called *records*) in tree structures. For example, a department could include records for the positions it contained and the equipment checked out to it. Each position, in turn, could be associated with a list of responsibilities and a list of employees in the department holding that position.

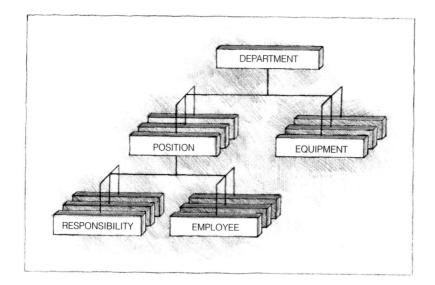

A more recent kind of database, the **network model**, allowed data to be interconnected freely, with no requirement that it fit into a tree structure. In the previous example, each piece of equipment could be associated with both a department and a list of employees who were authorized to use it. This kind of association would not be permitted in the hierarchic model.

The network model extended the hierarchic model

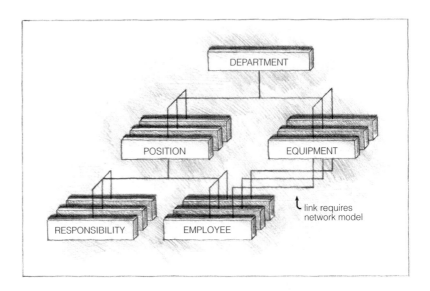

link requires network model

Fixed data structures reduce flexibility

The hierarchic and network database models made it easy to represent complex relationships among data elements, but there was a cost: accessing the data in a way other than the one supported by the predefined relationships was slow and inefficient. Worse yet, the data structures were hard to modify; changing these structures required system administrators to shut down the database and rebuild it.

The relational model removes most of the structure

A newer form of database manager, the **relational model**, addresses these problems by removing the information about complex relationships from the database. All data is stored in simple tables, with basic relationships among data items being expressed as references to values in other tables. For example, each entry in the equipment table would contain a value indicating which department it belonged to.

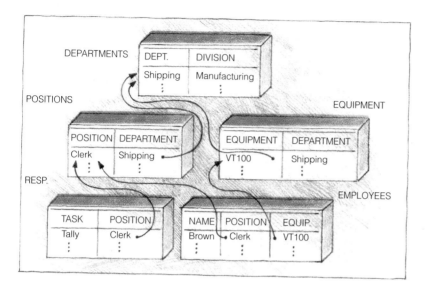

Although the relational model is much more flexible than its predecessors, it pays a price for this flexibility. The information about complex relationships that was removed from the database must be expressed as procedures in every program that accesses the database, a clear violation of the independence required for modularity. There is also a performance penalty because the original data structures must be reassembled every time the data is accessed.

Removing structure has costs, too

The Object-Oriented Approach

Despite all efforts to find better ways to build programs, the software crisis is growing worse with each passing year. Forty years after the invention of the subroutine, we are still building systems by hand, one instruction at a time. We've developed better methods for this construction process, but these methods don't work well in large systems. In addition, these methods usually produce defect-ridden software that's hard to modify and maintain.

None of these efforts has solved the software crisis

We need a new approach to building systems

We need a new approach to building software, one that leaves behind the bricks and mortar of conventional programming and offers a truly better way to construct systems. This new approach must be able to handle large systems as well as small, and it must create reliable systems that are flexible, maintainable, and capable of evolving to meet changing needs.

Object-oriented technology is the new approach

Object-oriented technology can meet these challenges and more. The remainder of this guide explains how this technology works and illustrates its potential to succeed where other methods have failed.

2

Three Keys to Object-Oriented Technology

This chapter introduces the three keys to understanding object-oriented technology – objects, messages, and classes. My goal in this chapter is to give you a general idea of how these basic ideas combine to form the object-oriented approach to software development. I will explain each of these ideas in greater depth in the succeeding three chapters.

This chapter provides a brief overview

One of the barriers to understanding object-oriented technology is the specialized vocabulary that has grown up around it. While some of this vocabulary is pure jargon, most of the terms are worth learning because they refer to concepts that are truly unique.

There are many new terms

Actually, it's possible to be quite conversant in "object-speak" using no more than ten basic terms: *object, method, message, class, subclass, instance, inheritance, encapsulation, abstraction,* and *polymorphism.* For your convenience, the appendix at the back of this guide defines these ten concepts. Also, terms introduced in boldface are defined in the glossary, so you can always turn to the back of the guide if you forget the meaning of a term.

But you can get by with just ten words if you like

Introducing Objects

Although object-oriented technology has come into the limelight only recently, it's actually more than twenty years old. Virtually all the basic concepts of the object-oriented approach were introduced in the **Simula** programming language developed in Norway during the late 1960s.

Simula was the first object-oriented language

Modeling Physical Objects

Simula was built to simulate real-world processes

Simula, an acronym for "simulation language," was created to support computer simulations of real-world processes. The authors of Simula, O. J. Dahl and Kristen Nygaard, wanted to build accurate working models of complex physical systems that could contain many thousands of components.

In Simula, modules are based on physical objects

It was apparent even back in the sixties that modular programming is essential for building complex systems, and modularization plays a central role in Simula. What's special about Simula is the way in which modules are defined. They are not based on procedures, as they are in conventional programming. In Simula, modules are based on the physical objects being modeled in the simulation.

This is a natural way to define modules

This choice makes a lot of sense because the objects in a simulation offer a very natural way of breaking down the problem to be solved. Each object has a range of behavior to be modeled, and each has to maintain some information about its own status. Why look for some other way to package procedures and data when the problem has already organized them for you?

Inside Objects

Software objects combine procedures and data

The concept of software objects arose out of the need to model real-world objects in computer simulations. An **object** is a software "package" that contains a collection of related procedures and data. In the object-oriented approach, procedures go by a special name; they are called **methods**. In keeping with traditional programming terminology, the data elements are referred to as **variables** because their values can vary over time.

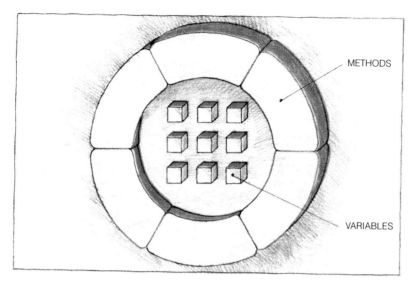

METHODS

VARIABLES

For example, consider how you might represent an automated guided vehicle (AGV) in the simulation of a factory. The vehicle can exhibit a variety of behaviors, such as moving from one location to another or loading and unloading its contents. It must also maintain information about both its inherent characteristics (pallet size, lifting capacity, maximum speed, and so on) and its current state (contents, location, orientation, and velocity).

Example: modeling an automated vehicle

To represent the vehicle as an object, you would describe its behaviors as methods and its characteristics as variables. During the simulation, the object would carry out its various methods, changing its variables as needed to reflect the effects of its actions.

Simulation involves actions and states

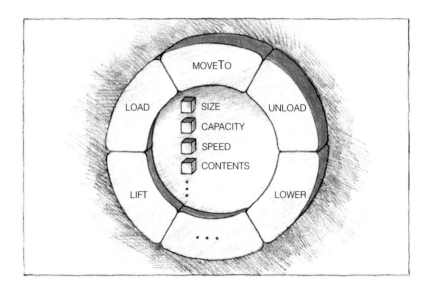

*Objects make excellent
software modules*

The concept of an object is simple yet powerful. Objects make ideal software modules because they can be defined and maintained independently of one another, with each object forming a neat, self-contained universe. Everything an object "knows" is expressed in its variables. Everything it can do is expressed in its methods.

Introducing Messages

*Objects can interact in
a rich variety of ways*

Real-world objects can exhibit an infinite variety of effects on each other – creating, destroying, lifting, attaching, buying, bending, sending, and so on. This tremendous variety raises an interesting problem – how can all these different kinds of interactions be represented in software?

The authors of Simula came up with an elegant solution to this problem: the message. The way objects interact with each other is to send each other messages asking them to carry out their methods. A **message** is simply the name of an object followed by the name of a method the object knows how to execute. If a method requires any additional information in order to know precisely what to do, the message includes that information as a collection of data elements called **parameters**. The object that initiates a message is called the **sender** and the object that receives the message is called the **receiver**.

These interactions are expressed as messages

To make an automated vehicle move to a new location, for example, some other object might send it the message:

Example: moving an automated vehicle

>   *vehicle104 moveTo binB7*

In this example, *vehicle104* is the name of the receiver, *moveTo* is the method it is being asked to execute, and *binB7* is a parameter telling the receiver where to go.

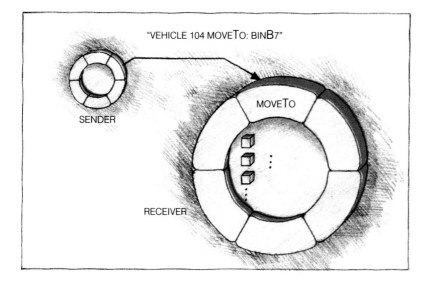

Message to
vehicle104

Messages support all possible interactions

An object-oriented simulation, then, consists of some number of objects interacting with each other by sending messages to one another. Since everything an object can do is expressed by its methods, this simple mechanism supports all possible interactions between objects.

Introducing Classes

There may be many objects of any given type

Sometimes a simulation involves only a single example of a particular kind of object. It is much more common, however, to need more than one object of each kind. An automated factory, for example, might have any number of guided vehicles. This possibility raises another concern: it would be extremely inefficient to redefine the same methods in every single occurrence of that object.

Creating Templates with Classes

Classes define groups of similar objects

Here again, the authors of Simula came up with an elegant solution: the class. A **class** is a template that defines the methods and variables to be included in a particular type of object. The descriptions of the methods and variables that support them are included only once, in the definition of the class. The objects that belong to a class, called **instances** of the class, contain only their particular values for the variables.

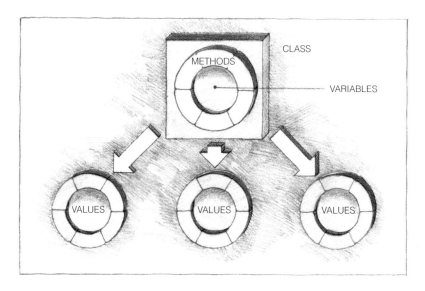

To continue the previous example, a simulated factory might contain many automated vehicles, each of which carried out the same actions and maintained the same kinds of information. The entire collection of vehicles could be represented by a class called *AutomatedVehicle*, and that class would contain the definitions of its methods and variables. The actual vehicles would be represented by instances of this class, each with its own unique name (*vehicle101, vehicle102, vehicle103…*). Each instance would contain data values which represented its own particular contents and location. When a vehicle received a message to carry out a method, it would turn to the class for the definition of that method and then apply the method to its own local data values.

Example: the auto-mated vehicle class

An object, then, is an instance of a particular class. Its methods and variables are defined in the class, and its values are defined in the instance. To keep my explanations simple, I usually talk about objects wherever possible, referring to classes and instances only when it's important to point out where the object's information is actually stored. For example, if I say that the object *vehicle104* has a method called *moveTo*, this is simply a more convenient way of saying that *vehicle104* is an instance of a class that defines a method called *moveTo*.

Objects are instances of classes

Inheriting Class Information

Classes can be defined in terms of each other

Simula took the concept of classes one step further by allowing classes to be defined in terms of each other. If you needed to represent two different kinds of automated vehicle, you could define one vehicle class in detail, then define the other as everything in the first one plus some additional methods and variables. This strategy was an early form of inheritance, a feature that has since become central to object-oriented technology.

Inheritance is the mechanism that allows this

Inheritance is a mechanism whereby one class of objects can be defined as a special case of a more general class, automatically including the method and variable definitions of the general class. Special cases of a class are known as **subclasses** of that class; the more general class, in turn, is known as the **superclass** of its special cases. In addition to the methods and variables they inherit, subclasses may define their own methods and variables and may override any of the inherited characteristics.

Subclasses of a superclass

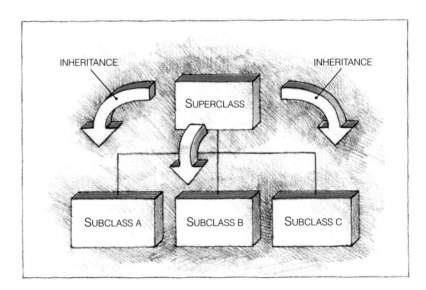

For example, the class *AutomatedVehicle* could be broken down into two subclasses, *PalletAGV* and *RollAGV*, each of which inherited the general characteristics of the parent class. Either subclass could establish its own special characteristics by adding to the parent's definition or by overriding its behavior.

Example: two types of automated vehicle

Two subclasses of automated vehicle

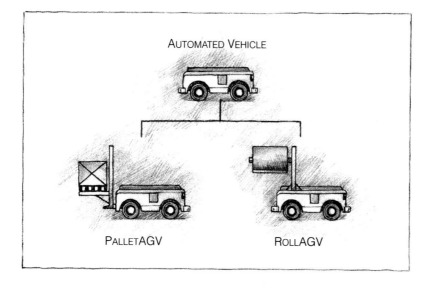

AUTOMATED VEHICLE

PALLETAGV   ROLLAGV

Hierarchies of Classes

Classes can be nested to any degree, and inheritance will automatically accumulate down through all the levels. The resulting treelike structure is known as a **class hierarchy**. A class called *Part*, for example, could be broken down into special kinds of parts such as *Motor, Chassis, Connector,* and so on. *Motor,* in turn, could be divided into *DriveMotor* and *SteppingMotor,* each of which could be broken down further as needed. An instance of, say, *VariableSpeedDriveMotor* would inherit all the characteristics of the *Part* class, as well as those of *Motor* and *DriveMotor.*

Complete hierarchies of classes can be built up

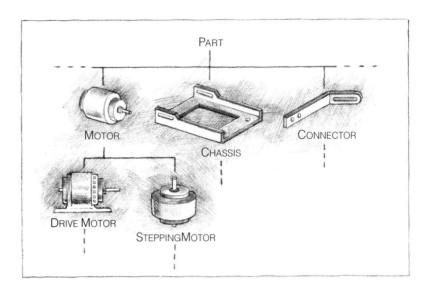

*Class hierarchies
reflect human
understanding*

The invention of the class hierarchy is the true genius of object-oriented technology. Human knowledge is structured in just this manner, relying on generic concepts and their refinement into increasingly specialized cases. Object-oriented technology uses the same conceptual mechanisms we employ in everyday life to build complex yet understandable software systems.

Programming with Objects

*There are now many
object-oriented
languages*

Objects, messages, and classes are the central mechanisms of object-oriented technology. Although Simula was never widely accepted as a general-purpose language, the concepts it spawned have spread to numerous languages over the past twenty years and have been implemented in a rich variety of ways. For the sake of simplicity, I will discuss only the two most important object-oriented languages in the remainder of this guide: Smalltalk and C++.

Two Example Languages

Smalltalk was developed in the early seventies at the Xerox research facility in Palo Alto, California, by a team of researchers led by Alan Kay. Smalltalk reflects the strategy of designing a totally new language to embrace the object-oriented approach. **C++** was developed in the early eighties at AT&T's Bell Laboratories by Bjarne Stroustrup. C++ is an extension to AT&T's popular C language, so it represents the strategy of grafting object-oriented concepts onto an existing language. The odd name, by the way, is a programmer's play on words. In C, the "++" operator increases a variable by one, so C++ represents the next step beyond C.

These languages reflect very different strategies

These two languages are the most widely used object-oriented languages today, and they illustrate two very different approaches to realizing the object-oriented vision. Smalltalk is generally regarded as one of the purest implementations to date of the object-oriented methodology, and it requires strict adherence to that methodology. C++ exemplifies the so-called hybrid approach, in which conventional language features coexist with object-oriented features. Unlike Smalltalk, C++ allows considerable latitude in conforming to the object-oriented methodology, a quality that some regard as an important advantage and others as a serious flaw.

Smalltalk is "pure" and C++ is "hybrid"

Software as Simulation

Traditionally, software has been viewed as a way to make a computer perform a particular task. This view is reflected in the overall progression of software development projects: they begin with a specification of the problem to be solved, followed by a design for a system that produces the required behavior, and so on. Typically, the result is a system that performs the original task but is ill-suited for handling other tasks – even when they deal with the same real-world objects. A billing system is a billing system, and it's not about to handle mailings for the marketing department or ticklers for the sales team.

Conventional software solves a specific problem

Object-oriented software models a system

There is a different mindset underlying object-oriented technology. Although the technology has spread far beyond its origins as a simulation language, programming with objects still retains the spirit of real-world simulation. The design of an object-oriented system begins not with the task to be performed, but rather with the aspects of the real world that need to be modeled in order to perform that task. Once these are correctly represented, the model can be used to solve a wide variety of tasks, including the original one. If you have a good model of your customers and your interactions with them, you can use this model equally well for billings, mailings, and ticklers.

Using models has many advantages

The object-oriented approach to building software systems has many other advantages besides flexibility. Because the structure of the software reflects the real world, programmers can more easily understand and modify it in the future even if they aren't the same people who built the software in the first place. More importantly, the basic operations of a company tend to change much more slowly than the information needs of specific groups or individuals. This means that software based on corporate models will have a much longer life span than programs written to solve specific, immediate problems.

Programming as Object Assembly

Conventional software is usually built from scratch

The process by which software is constructed is very different in the object-oriented approach. Most conventional software is still written from scratch, with very little reuse of procedures from earlier programs. Because these programs are written to solve very specific problems, it's usually easier to write new procedures than to convert existing ones.

Objects, by contrast, are general-purpose building blocks that model real-world entities rather than performing specific tasks. This makes them easy to reuse in subsequent projects, even if the objectives of the new projects are quite different. As more and more classes are accumulated, the software development effort begins to shift from creating new classes of objects to assembling existing ones in new ways. A mature object-oriented development team may devote as little as twenty percent of its time to creating new classes. The majority of its time is spent assembling proven components into new systems.

Object-oriented systems are built by assembly

The Promise of the Approach

There is much more to the object-oriented approach than I have covered in this brief introduction, but some of the promise of this new way of thinking should now be apparent. Object-oriented technology offers some powerful techniques for creating flexible, natural software modules. Moreover, the focus on building general-purpose models produces systems that are much easier to adapt to new demands. Finally, the extensive reuse of existing, proven components not only shortens development time, it also leads to more robust, error-free systems.

The approach has many important advantages

Each of these benefits will play a crucial role in resolving the software crisis we now face.

All are essential

3

Objects: Natural Building Blocks

Object-oriented programming is often said to be more natural than traditional programming, and this is true on a couple of different levels. On one level, object-oriented programming is more natural because it allows us to organize information in ways that are familiar to us. On a deeper level, it is more natural in that it reflects nature's own techniques for managing complexity. A brief digression into the structure of living organisms will provide important insights into the power of objects.

The object-oriented approach is more natural

Nature's Building Blocks

The basic building block out of which all living things are composed is the cell. Cells are organic "packages" that, like objects, combine related information and behavior. Most of the information is contained in protein molecules within the nucleus of the cell. The behavior, which may range from energy conversion to movement, is carried out by structures outside the nucleus.

Cells encapsulate data and behavior

A living cell

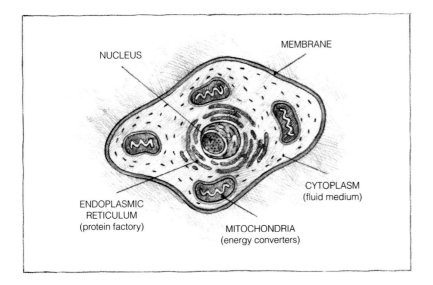

NUCLEUS

MEMBRANE

ENDOPLASMIC
RETICULUM
(protein factory)

MITOCHONDRIA
(energy converters)

CYTOPLASM
(fluid medium)

Cells communicate through messages

Cells are surrounded by a membrane that permits only certain kinds of chemical exchanges with other cells. This membrane not only protects the internal workings of the cell from outside intrusion, it also hides the complexity of the cell and presents a relatively simple interface to the rest of the organism. All interactions between cells take place through chemical messages recognized by the cell membrane and passed through to the inside of the cell.

This simplifies the interactions between cells

This message-based communication greatly simplifies the way cells function. The cells don't have to read each others' protein molecules or control each others' structures to get what they need from each other – all they do is broadcast the appropriate chemical message and the receiving cell responds accordingly.

Living cells are ideal building blocks

The cell is truly a universal building block. All cells share a common structure and operate according to the same basic principles. Within this basic structure, however, infinite variability is possible – plant cells have a hard outer wall to make them rigid, blood cells are mobile and specialized to transport gases, muscle cells are able to distort their shape to perform mechanical work, and so on. But this tremendous variability is not chaotic; it's all neatly organized – or "classified" – in a hierarchy of specialized types and subtypes.

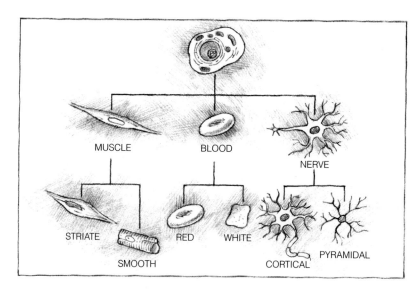

Objects, as defined in object-oriented technology, have many of the essential characteristics of living cells. A closer look inside the structure of an object reveals some of these similarities.

Objects are like cells

The Anatomy of an Object

Packaging related data and procedures together is called **encapsulation**. As you can see from the structure of a cell, encapsulation is an idea that's been around for a very long time. The fact that it has worked so well in natural systems suggests that we may, in fact, be on the right track with this mechanism!

Placing data with behavior is called encapsulation

Hiding Information

The encapsulation mechanism of object-oriented technology is a natural extension of the information-hiding strategy developed in structured programming. Object-oriented technology improves on this strategy with better mechanisms to pull the right kinds of information together and hide their details more effectively.

Encapsulation promotes information hiding

In the object-oriented approach, the data inside an object is accessed only by the object's methods. That's why the illustrations in the last chapter showed objects as an inner core of variables surrounded by an outer shell of methods. Just as cells don't "read" each other's protein molecules, objects don't touch each others' data structures. Rather, objects send each other messages that call methods into action. These methods, in turn, access the required variables.

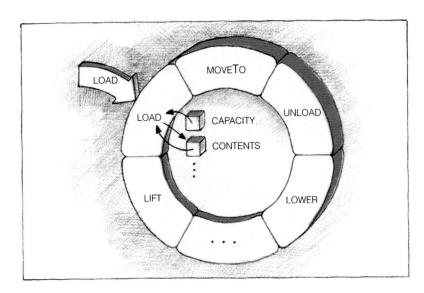

This message-based communication offers two important kinds of protection. First, it protects an object's variables from being corrupted by other objects. If other objects had direct access to an object's variables, eventually one of them would handle a variable incorrectly and damage the object. An object protects itself from this kind of error by hiding its variables and accessing them only through its own methods.

The second and less obvious kind of protection works in the opposite direction – by hiding its variables, an object protects other objects from the complications of depending on its internal structure. They are spared having to keep track of each variable's name, the type of information it contains, the amount of space it takes up in storage, and a host of other details that would complicate all their procedures for accessing those variables. With encapsulation, an object only needs to know how to ask another object for information. All the details about how that information is stored are neatly tucked out of sight.

It also protects outside objects from the data

Facilitating Changes

Encapsulation not only simplifies the interactions between objects, it also pays big dividends when you modify the way an object carries out its tasks.

Encapsulation really pays off with changes

Suppose that an automated vehicle object has a collection of methods to estimate its carrying capacity for various kinds of loads. After the system has been in use for a few months, its designers might decide that some of these estimates are not as accurate as they would like. So they could modify the object to store and retrieve actual measured capacities for the most common kinds of loads rather than calculating estimates.

Example: changing the automated vehicle

In a conventional system, this change would require a major restructuring. You would need to rewrite all the subroutines dealing with carrying capacities so they would retrieve stored capacities for certain kinds of loads and estimate the capacities for others. With encapsulation, the effects of the change are limited to a single class. The rest of the objects in the system simply ask for capacity values and get back answers, just as they always did.

Encapsulation limits this change to a single object

The Power of Abstract Data Types

Data abstraction
raises thinking to
a higher level

One of the key advantages of the object-oriented approach is that it allows you to think at the level of a real-world system, not at the level of a programming language. This elevation of the thought process is possible because you can define new kinds of data structures to describe real-world objects.

Abstract Data Types

Older languages
limited data to
built-in types

Traditionally, programming languages have strictly limited the kinds of data a program could operate on. Each language provided a fixed set of built-in **data types** for common kinds of variables, and programmers had to define all their variables in terms of these basic types.

This put problem
solving on the
wrong level

To be fair, these data types were fairly extensive, including types for large numbers, small numbers, dollar amounts, dates, and many other kinds of data. But they all shared an important limiting characteristic – they were defined by the way information is stored in the computer, and they bore no useful relationship to the real-world objects that programs ultimately deal with. Because programmers couldn't extend this fixed set of types, they were forced to think at the level of data storage rather than at the level of the problems they were trying to solve. In short, they would find themselves worrying about whether a number was likely to be small or large rather than whether a purchase order was approved or disapproved.

Modern computer languages have released programmers from the straightjacket of fixed data types. Programmers can define new data types, called **abstract data types**, by combining existing data types in new ways. The process of creating these new data types is known as **data abstraction**, a term that neatly reflects what's actually going on in this process. When you abstract something, you pull out its essential characteristics and package them in a more convenient, compact form. For example, a programmer could create a new data type to represent a purchase order, then deal directly with that purchase order in future operations.

Modern languages allow new data types to be added

Although many computer languages now support data abstraction, they share a common limitation: they don't treat the programmer-defined data types the same way they treat the built-in types. Many services provided to the built-in types are unavailable to the abstract types, forcing the programmer to write new procedures to provide these services.

Abstract types are usually second-class citizens

Objects as Abstract Data Types

Object-oriented technology provides extensive support for data abstraction. The technology not only allows a programmer to create new data types on the fly, it actually treats these new types as though they had been built into the language. In fact, object-oriented languages are specifically designed to be extended and adapted to specialized needs. This process of extending the language is not just encouraged, it's the very essence of object-oriented programming!

Object technology is based on abstract data types

The tool for creating new data types is the class. At its simplest, an abstract data type consists of a new class assembled from built-in data types, such as numbers and characters.

Data types are added by defining new classes

A simple abstract data type

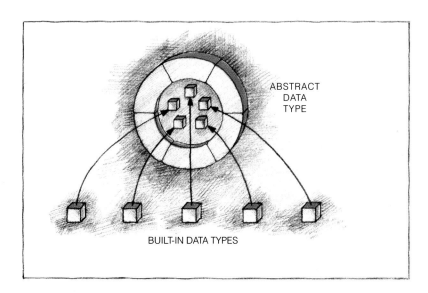

ABSTRACT
DATA
TYPE

BUILT-IN DATA TYPES

Example: purchase orders as data types

In a system that deals with purchase orders, for example, you can define a new data type to represent purchase orders directly. This new data type enjoys all the rights and privileges of the built-in data types, including access to specialized computing operations. Just as numbers can be added, subtracted, and so on, purchase orders can be combined, split, and manipulated in other ways. Once you define the purchase-order object, the language acts as though it had always known how to handle purchase orders.

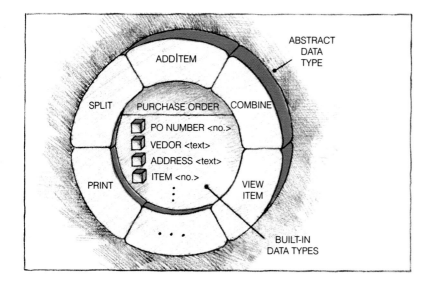

ABSTRACT
DATA
TYPE

ADDITEM

SPLIT   PURCHASE ORDER   COMBINE

PO NUMBER <no.>

VEDOR <text>

ADDRESS <text>

ITEM <no.>

PRINT   VIEW
                               ITEM

BUILT-IN
DATA TYPES

Composite Objects for High-Level Abstractions

In the purchase-order example, all the variables contain basic data types such as numbers and characters. There is, however, another kind of information that variables can contain; namely, other objects.

Objects can also contain other objects

Objects that contain other objects are called **composite objects**. Composite objects are important because they can represent far more sophisticated structures than simple objects can. For example, an aircraft consists of wings, engines, and other components far too complex to be represented as simple numbers or text.

This increases their representational power

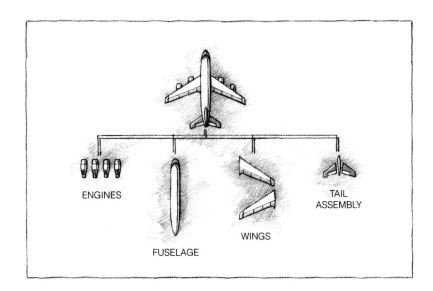

ENGINES

TAIL
ASSEMBLY

WINGS

FUSELAGE

*Composite objects
can be nested*

The objects contained in composite objects may themselves be composite
objects, and this "nesting" can be carried out to any number of levels.
The major components of an aircraft, for example, are all very complex
objects in their own right. In any reasonable simulation, each of these
components would be represented by composite objects which, in all
likelihood, would be composed of still more composite objects, and so on.

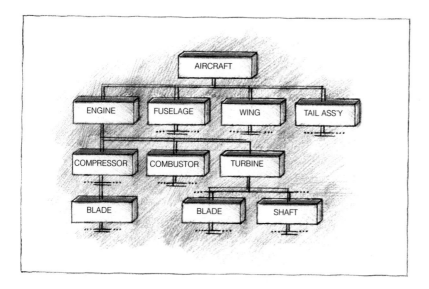

Because objects can be composed of other objects, object-oriented languages can represent information in the way we naturally think about it. Even a complex, deeply nested structure can be treated as a single, unified object. And since that complex object can have its own behavior, other objects can use it with very little awareness of its internal complexity. This approach not only keeps simple things simple, it can make complex things simple as well.

*Composition permits
high-level abstractions*

The Ideal of Organic Systems

Although the actual mechanics of cells and objects differ dramatically, their overall functions are remarkably similar. Both cells and objects encapsulate associated data and behavior, both make use of message-based communication to hide complexity, both appear in a hierarchy of specialized types, and both provide the fundamental building blocks for constructing an infinite variety of complex systems.

*Cells and objects are
strikingly similar*

This similarity is encouraging – the incredible variation among living organisms clearly indicates the flexibility of this basic approach to constructing complex systems. Moreover, pursuing the analogy could lead to important insights into the problems of software construction. Nature, after all, has been using the approach a few billion years longer than software developers have!

*Example: organs
and systems*

Here's a case in point: the cell is only the most basic level of modularization in complex organisms. The higher levels include organs and systems, such as the heart and the circulatory system. We will surely need corresponding levels of modularity in our software systems as they move toward the scale and complexity of living organisms. Composite objects will be an important tool in defining those high-level modules.

**Cells, organs, and
systems**

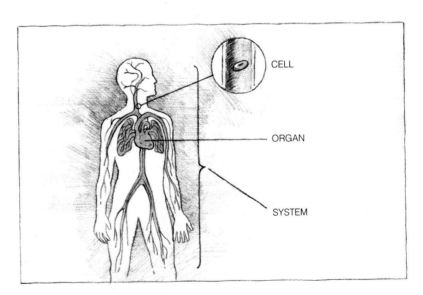

4

Messages: Activating Objects

However carefully crafted, an object is useless in isolation; its value comes from its interactions with other objects. The vehicle for these interactions is the message.

Objects interact through messages

The Anatomy of a Message

A message consists of three parts: the name of a receiving object, the name of a method the receiver knows how to execute, and any parameters that this method requires to carry out its function. The third part is optional; if the method doesn't need any additional information, there are no parameters in the message.

A message has three parts

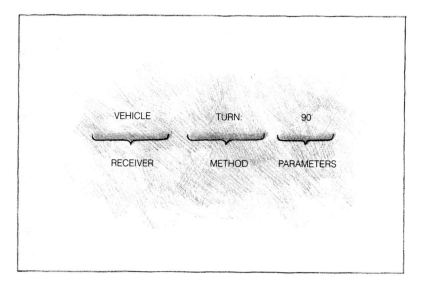

The structure of a message

This is the basic structure of a message. Within this structure there is room for considerable variation.

This structure can vary

How Messages Are Written

Message format varies from language to language

The way a message is written depends on the language you're using. Typically, the three components of the message appear in a fixed order – receiver + method + parameters – but the way you name the components and separate them from each other tends to vary. A message in Smalltalk, for example, might look like this:

vehicle104 turn: 90

The same message in C++ would look like this:

vehicle104.turn(90)

In each case, *vehicle104* is the name of the receiving object, *turn* is the method the receiver is being asked to execute, and *90* is a parameter that specifies the angle of rotation.

Most examples will use the Smalltalk format

In the following examples I've used the Smalltalk format because it's closer to natural English. But be aware that Smalltalk does have a rather puzzling quirk; it requires that class names be capitalized and instances begin with lower case letters. That's backwards from English, which capitalizes the names of specific instances – we write "a man named John," not "a Man named john" as Smalltalk would have it. Oh, well; just remember that any word starting with a capital letter is a class.

The format may also vary with type of message

The basic message format is quite flexible and may take some surprising appearances, such as this one:

age + 10

In this case, the object named *age* is being sent the message + with the parameter *10*, causing it to add ten to its current value. As it happens, *age* is an instance of the class *Number* and all numbers know how to carry out simple arithmetic methods such as addition and subtraction.

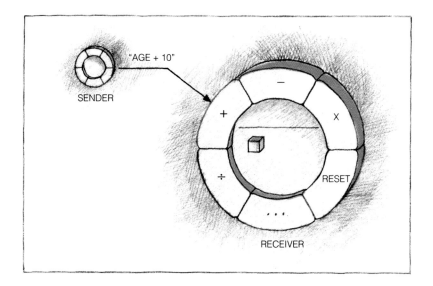

Responses to Messages

Messages are usually two-way communications. The primary communication is a request from the sender of a message to the receiver. But the sender may also require a response from the receiver. At the very least, the sender may need some confirmation that the receiver was, in fact, able to carry out the desired action.

Messages usually require some feedback

This response is usually called a *return value*. Return values can take different forms, depending on the language. In pure languages like Smalltalk, a message always returns an object to the sender. In hybrid languages like C++, a message can return either an object or a simple variable.

This response is called a return value

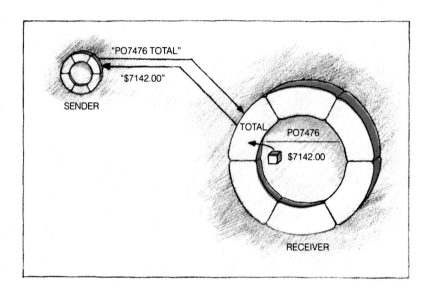

Reusing Names

Within a program, any given task may be carried out in a variety of different ways. This situation raises an important question concerning the name of the task: can you use the same name for all the variations, or do you have to use a different name for each? The question is important because a large program can contain so many different names that it's nearly impossible to keep track of them all. Keeping the number of different names to a minimum simplifies the programming process and makes programs more understandable.

Overloading Names

Consider an electronic drawing program in which you can draw a variety of different shapes on the display screen. A conventional programming language would require that the software commands to draw these shapes all have unique names: *drawPoint, drawLine, drawRectangle, drawCircle*, and so on. Depending on the number of shapes, the drawing program could require a great many different names for the drawing command.

In an object-oriented system, each kind of shape would be represented by a different class. Through a technique called **overloading**, you can use the same name for the drawing method in every class. Although the actual method is different in each class – *drawPoint* vs. *drawLine*, for example – all the different methods are called *draw*. Because each class knows only about its own version of *draw*, there's no possibility of confusion within the program.

Overloading solves this problem

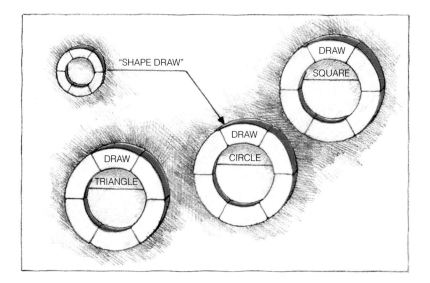

A draw method in multiple objects

Overloading simplifies programs because it allows you to use the same name for the same operation everywhere in a program. It's up to the receiving object to carry out the operation in its own unique way. Name overloading also simplifies the way in which objects request services from each other because they can use the same message for an entire family of objects.

Overloading simplifies programs

The *draw* method illustrates this point nicely. If you could not reuse names across objects, then asking a particular kind of shape to draw itself would be a rather complicated process. If the shape were a *Rectangle*, the *drawRectangle* message would have to be sent; if it were a *Circle*, the *drawCircle* message would be required, and so on. In short, the simple act of asking a shape to draw itself would require a complete list of all the different shapes in the system together with the names of each of their drawing operations. And this list would have to be duplicated in every object that could ever ask a shape to draw itself.

```
         ⋮
IF SHAPE = CIRCLE THEN
    SHAPE DRAWCIRCLE
ELSE IF SHAPE = SQUARE THEN
    SHAPE DRAWSQUARE
ELSE IF SHAPE = OVAL THEN
    SHAPE DRAWOVAL
ELSE IF SHAPE = TRIANGLE THEN
    SHAPE DRAWTRIANGLE
ELSE IF SHAPE = RECTANGLE THEN
    SHAPE DRAWRECTANGLE
         ⋮

ETC.
         ⋮
```

Adding a new shape
would require major
changes

This is an ugly prospect, but it gets even uglier when a new shape is added to the system. Every class that sends drawing messages has to be modified to include the new shape and send the appropriate command. Multiply this problem by all the different kinds of interactions objects can have with shapes and this slight extension of the program winds up requiring a major reconstruction.

Overloading as Information Hiding

This example is yet another illustration of the importance of information hiding. The problem here is that the objects in this program know too much about each other.

The problem is neatly overcome through overloading. If all shape classes use the same name for their drawing operation, none of the other classes has to keep track of the various names for this operation in order to send each shape the correct one. A class can send the same *draw* message to all the shapes in the system and trust that each will handle it in the appropriate way. Overloading eliminates all the instructions that were required to figure out which drawing message to send. This simplifies the program dramatically.

Objects shouldn't know too much about each other

Overloading reduces the information load

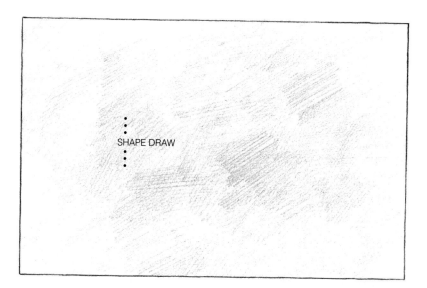

SHAPE DRAW

Sending a generic draw message

Overloading is even more useful when you add a new shape. The new shape would implement its own *draw* method, using the same name as all the other shapes. Whenever another object wants this new shape to draw itself, the object simply sends the generic *draw* message, just as it does with any other shape. In fact, existing objects don't even need to know that a new shape has been added; they're totally unaffected by the change. You can add a new shape simply by declaring a new class of objects, without rebuilding the program to accommodate it.

The Power of Polymorphism

Hiding alternative procedures behind a common interface is called **polymorphism**, a Greek term meaning "many forms." Polymorphism is so important that it's considered one of the defining characteristics of object-oriented technology. The key benefits of polymorphism are that it makes objects more independent of each other and allows new objects to be added with minimal changes to existing objects. These benefits, in turn, lead to much simpler systems that are far more capable of evolving over time to meet changing needs.

All this from the simple ability to use the same method name in more than one class!

5

Classes: Bringing Order to Objects

Objects communicating through messages form the essence of object-oriented technology. These two mechanisms alone could provide the basis for a powerful programming language. In fact, the *Ada* language used by the Department of Defense is built on precisely these mechanisms. But it's the concept of classes that brings order to the object-oriented approach and makes it so efficient for representing complex information.

Classes organize the object-oriented approach

In the same way that a classification system brings order to an otherwise bewildering array of plants and animals, classes allow a programmer to organize complex systems in a rational, orderly way. And just as mutations in a couple of genes can lead to a new kind of insect, so can changes in a couple of methods create a new subclass that automatically inherits all the characteristics of its parent class.

And they allow complex systems to evolve

The Anatomy of a Class

The Basic Division of Labor

The basic function of a class is to define a particular type of object. Once you've defined a class, you can create any number of unique instances of the class. The class defines the characteristics shared by all the instances, whereas the instances themselves contain the information that makes them unique.

Classes define common characteristics of objects

The only aspects of a class that differ from one instance to the next are the values of its variables, so an instance actually consists of nothing more than a sequence of slots to hold values. When an instance receives a message, it looks to its class for its methods and variable types and then applies these to its own unique set of values.

Instances contain only the values of variables

A concrete example will clarify this division of labor. Suppose an automated vehicle object receives the following message:

vehicle104 moveTo: binB7

The object *vehicle104* would look up the *moveTo:* method in its class, *AutomatedVehicle*, and execute that method. The *moveTo:* method, in turn, might need to check the current location of *vehicle104*. The method would identify the appropriate variable within the class, then take the value for it from the instance *vehicle104*.

Vehicle104's class
and instance

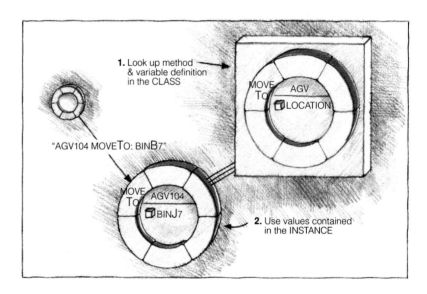

1. Look up method & variable definition in the CLASS

MOVE To AGV LOCATION

"AGV104 MOVETO: BINB7"

MOVE To AGV104 BINJ7

2. Use values contained in the INSTANCE

How an Object Finds a Method or Variable

When an object receives a message to carry out a method that isn't de-fined in its class, the object automatically searches up the class hierarchy to find the method. First, the object looks in the immediate superclass of its class. If the method isn't defined there, the object looks in the super-class of the superclass, and so on. If it finds a definition for the method, the object executes it. If the object gets all the way to the top of the class hierarchy without finding the method, it responds with an error message. In effect, the object tells the sender, "I'd like to help you out, but I can't figure out what you want."

An object will search its superclasses for methods

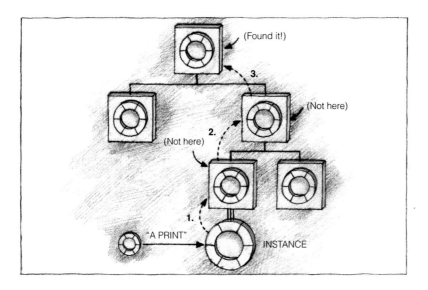

Searching up the hierarchy

Objects use this same process to locate variables as well. Before an object can operate on one of its values, it must find the definition of the corre-sponding variable. The object will search up the entire class hierarchy for the variable and respond with an error message if it fails. This arrange-ment is very flexible because a method defined at one level of the class hierarchy can operate on a variable defined on another level using a value stored on yet another level!

It performs the same kind of search for variables

The class hierarchy is a very efficient mechanism because you can use method and variable definitions in more than one subclass without duplicating their definitions. For example, consider a system which represents various kinds of human-operated vehicles. This system would contain a generic class for vehicles, with subclasses for all the specialized types. The *Vehicle* class would contain the methods and variables that were pertinent to all vehicles – dealing, say, with identification numbers, passenger loads, and fuel capacity. The subclasses, in turn, would contain any additional methods and variables that were specific to the individual cases.

Subclasses of the vehicle class

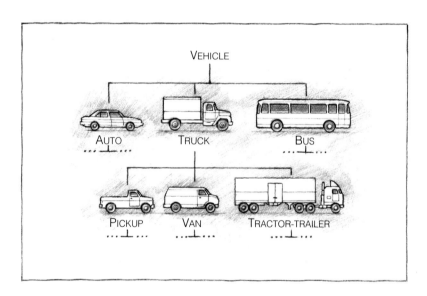

The flexibility and efficiency of inheritance isn't free; it takes time to search a class hierarchy to find a method or variable, so an object-oriented program could run slower than its conventional counterpart. However, language designers have developed techniques to eliminate this speed penalty in most cases by allowing classes to link directly to their inherited methods and variables so that no searching is actually required. The result is the best of both worlds: programs appear to conduct the level-by-level searches described above, but methods and variables are accessed without the overhead of an actual search.

Relationships Among Classes

Favoring the Exception

Although methods are normally defined at only one level of a class hierarchy – the level at which they apply most generally – there is nothing to prevent a method from being defined at a general level and also at a more specific level. In this case, objects would always use the more specific definition because that definition would be the first one found in the hierarchy search.

Methods can be defined on multiple levels

The ability to define methods on more than one level is used to create exceptions to general rules. Suppose you have a *Vehicle* class that includes a method *scheduleMaintenance* for setting up maintenance work based on time, mileage, and other factors. At a later date, your company acquires a private aircraft, so you create a new subclass of *Vehicle* to handle aircraft. But now you have a problem; scheduling maintenance for an aircraft is an entirely different process from the procedure you've been using for all your ground-based vehicles.

This technique is useful for defining exceptions

Adding an aircraft subclass

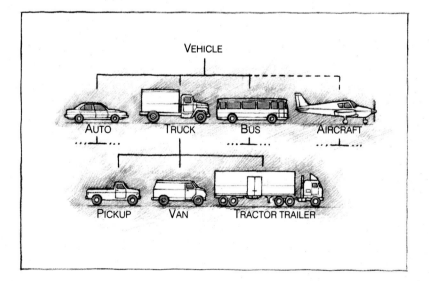

53

One way to fix your class hierarchy would be to move the *schedule-Maintenance* method down a level into the subclasses for the various types of vehicle. But this approach would require you to modify the *Vehicle* class and all of its subclasses. More importantly, all but one of the vehicle classes would wind up containing identical methods for scheduling maintenance, and that wouldn't be very efficient.

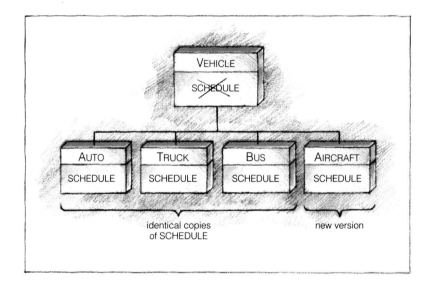

A better way to fix the hierarchy is just to redefine *scheduleMaintenance* in the *Aircraft* class to handle its special maintenance needs. Then you have only two versions of the method; one in the *Vehicle* class that handles the general case, and the other down in the *Aircraft* class that handles the one exception. Not only is this solution more efficient, it also doesn't require you to make any changes to your existing classes. And if you later change the way maintenance is scheduled for ground vehicles, you only have to modify the method in one location.

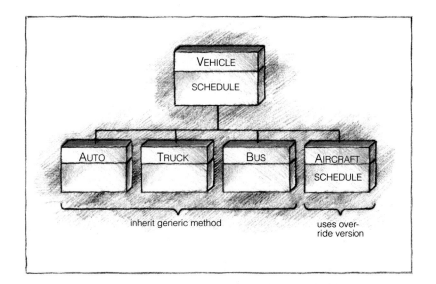

This technique of redefining a method in a subclass is another example of overloading, where the same method name is used in two different classes. In this particular case, one of the classes is a subclass of the other. The technique is often called **overriding** because the method in the subclass overrides the more general version.

This is a special case of overloading

Overriding is an important technique because it allows special cases to be handled efficiently and easily, with minimal impact on other objects. This technique also happens to reflect the way people learn and retain information, building up general rules wherever possible and then overriding them with special cases as needed. This is yet another way in which the object-oriented approach conforms to our natural way of looking at the world.

Overriding mirrors the way people learn

Virtual Classes

Some classes are
purely organizational

The ability to capture general cases in high-level classes is so useful that designers of object-oriented systems often define high-level classes purely for organizational purposes, even though no instances of those classes will ever exist. Such classes are sometimes called **abstract classes**, but that term invites confusion with the concept of abstract data types. I prefer the less ambiguous term **virtual class**.

Example: the class
of vehicles

The *Vehicle* class discussed above is an example of a virtual class. There are no instances of *Vehicle* per se; anything that would qualify as a vehicle is actually an *Automobile*, a *Truck*, an *Aircraft*, or some other particular type of vehicle. But defining a general class of vehicles brings a higher level of organization to the class hierarchy, and it provides a convenient place to put all the methods and variables that apply to vehicles as a group.

Multiple Inheritance

Some languages
permit multiple
superclasses

Strictly speaking, the kind of inheritance I've described so far is called **single inheritance** because each class has at most one superclass. In many object-oriented languages, such as Smalltalk, that's the only kind of inheritance there is. Other languages, including C++, permit a second kind of inheritance. It's called **multiple inheritance**, and it allows an object to have more than one superclass.

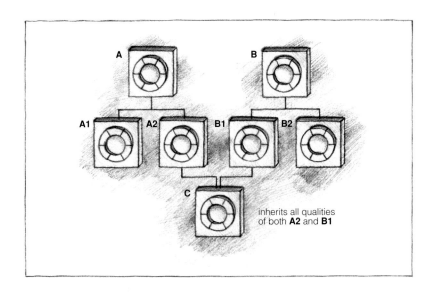

inherits all qualities
of both **A2** and **B1**

Multiple inheritance comes into play when a class of objects has to play multiple roles, and each of those roles is characterized by some other class. A foreman, for example, may play a dual role, functioning both as a supervisor and as a welder. With single inheritance, there is no way to combine the characteristics of the two job categories, supervisor and welder, without a lot of wasteful duplication. If *WelderForeman* is defined as a special case of *Welder*, then the characteristics of the class *Supervisor* have to be duplicated in the foreman subclass for every job description. A similar problem arises if *WelderForeman* is defined as a special case of *Supervisor*.

Multiple inheritance is used for multiple roles

With multiple inheritance, *WelderForeman* can be declared as a subclass of both supervisor and welder, inheriting all the qualities of each. The characteristics of *Supervisor* are defined in only one place, making them easier to program and maintain, and the same is true for the characteristics of *Welder*. And the definition of *WelderForeman* is a model of simplicity; all it contains are the names of its two superclasses.

This makes class definitions much simpler

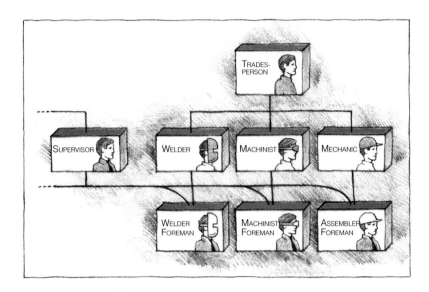

*Multiple inheritance
can complicate matters*

Although multiple inheritance can simplify certain situations, it can also lead to complications. For example, suppose both *Supervisor* and *Welder* contained a method called *reportStatus*. Then a *WelderForeman* would inherit two different versions of this method. Which one should it use? There are ways of dealing with this problem, but none of them is entirely satisfactory.

**Conflicting method
definitions**

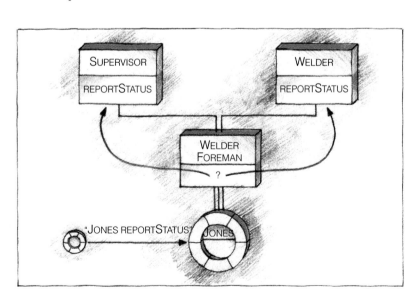

Another problem with multiple inheritance is that it's often misused. To apply multiple inheritance correctly, you must be certain that an object is truly an example of two or more classes. For example, the preceding illustration assumes that a *WelderForeman* really is a welder and spends time on the line performing that task. If this were not true – if the foreman supervised welders but didn't actually do any welding – then inheriting the qualities of *Welder* would not be appropriate.

Multiple inheritance is often misused

Given these complications, many authorities question whether the benefits of multiple inheritance outweigh its potential costs. The trend in object-oriented development products appears to be toward supporting multiple inheritance, but it's definitely a feature that should be used judiciously.

The feature should be used judiciously

Building Class Hierarchies

The great power of the class hierarchy is that it applies general rules to broad groups of objects while also accommodating exceptions to these rules. Because of the way an object-oriented system locates the definition of a method, the system will always apply the most specialized definition. It's hard to imagine a scheme that could offer a better combination of efficiency and flexibility.

The class hierarchy is a powerful device

Some languages, such as Smalltalk, are constructed with a single hierarchy for the entire system, with all classes ultimately converging on a generic class called *Object*. This structure is usually mandated because the system provides services at the highest level that must be available to all objects. Smalltalk, for example, uses the *Object* class to handle messages lower-level classes can't understand, and to delete objects that are no longer required.

Some languages permit only a single hierarchy

Other languages, such as C++, allow you to define any number of hierarchies. While you still have the option of defining a top-level class, you aren't required to do so. For example, you may find it more convenient to use multiple hierarchies if you are mixing classes from different sources that do not share any higher-level services.

**Multiple class
hierarchies**

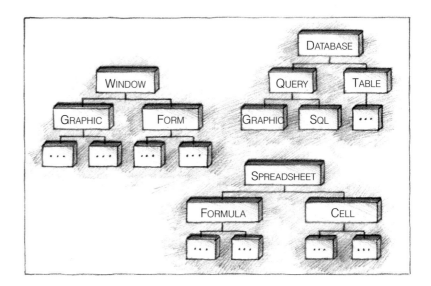

Several high-level goals should guide the development of class hierarchies. First, classes should be as general purpose as possible so that they can be reused easily; this approach makes the assembly method of programming possible. Second, methods should be defined at the highest possible level, even if they have to be overridden in special cases; this strategy not only eliminates redundancy, it makes changes much easier because a single modification is automatically "broadcast" to all the subclasses. Third, the class hierarchy should accurately reflect the structure of the real-world system it models, enhancing everyone's understanding of that system.

This last goal is the most subtle one. Traditionally, programming has been designed to solve specific, individual problems. While this approach may sometimes lead to quick solutions, it virtually guarantees that each new problem will have to be solved from scratch. The goal of object-oriented programming is just the opposite – to build solid, working models that can be used to solve any number of related problems. The solutions these models support will only be as good as the thinking that went into them.

Building a good working model is essential

6

A New Generation of Databases

Beating the software crisis requires more than a better way to build soft-ware – it calls for new techniques to manage information as well. The volume of information maintained by organizations has exploded over the last decade, and the information itself has become far more varied and complex. Information systems of the past needed only to store text and numbers in simple tabular form. Today's information systems must handle spreadsheets, images, diagrams, maps, voice records, and a wide variety of other multimedia data. And all of it has to be tied together into useful, high-level structures.

Information manage-ment is in crisis

Object-oriented technology has the potential to transform the way we store and retrieve information, solving these problems and adding a new dimension to the discipline of information management. The applications of object-oriented technology to database management fall into three broad categories: supporting object-oriented programs, storing complex information, and building intelligent databases. I'll explore each of these applications in turn.

Object-oriented tech-nology can help

Preserving Objects

Object-oriented programs rarely throw their objects away when the pro-gram stops running. Much more commonly, the program builds and maintains objects over time, reusing them whenever the program runs. But where are the objects kept? Where do objects go when their pro-grams aren't running?

Most programs need to store objects between runs

Storing Objects in Files

Smalltalk objects can be stored in image files

Smalltalk has a unique solution to the problem of preserving objects between runs; it stores the entire state of the system – including all the current objects, all the information on the screen, and any pending instructions to the system – in a special file called an **image file**. Smalltalk does this automatically whenever you exit from the system. When you return, Smalltalk reads the image file and restores the system to its previous state.

This is a convenient but limited solution

This type of data storage is elegant and convenient, but it's designed primarily for individuals working with stand-alone programs. The arrangement doesn't work too well for programs that share objects because it's difficult to exchange objects between image files.

Objects are more often stored in data files

The more common way to store objects is to keep them in data files. A program transfers the contents of its objects out to a file as part of its shutdown procedure, then loads them back in again the next time it is run. In effect, the program disassembles the objects to pack them into the data file, then reassembles them when the program resumes. Because any program can read the data file, this type of data storage makes it easier for programs to share objects.

Storing objects in data files

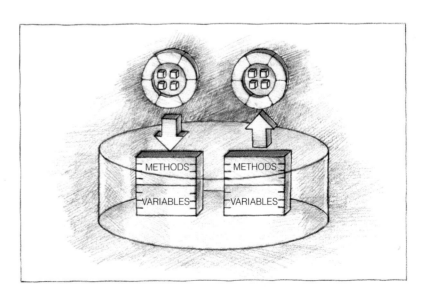

Storing Objects in Databases

Storing objects in data files works fine so long as no two people need to access the objects at the same time. Otherwise, conflicts can arise because the system can't check on who is working with which objects at any given moment. In addition, the data files have no security mechanisms to control access to the objects, and no procedures for protecting the objects against loss. These are the same concerns that led to the development of database managers for storing conventional data, and the conclusion is the same in the case of objects – shared objects must be maintained by a database management system.

Sharing objects requires a database manager

There is, however, a small problem with this conclusion: conventional database management systems were designed to store simple built-in data types such as text and numbers. These systems have no provision for handling the infinite variety of data types that object-oriented languages permit, and they were never intended to store the methods that objects contain.

But a conventional database manager won't work

Trying to store objects in a standard database

One approach to solving this problem is to put a layer of software above a database management system that converts complex objects into simpler components that conventional databases can deal with. When the objects are taken back out of the database, the software would convert them back into object form.

**Storing object
components**

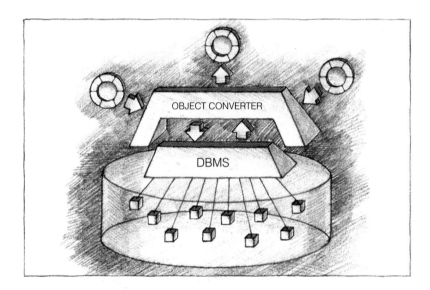

*Hierarchic and network models are
not well suited*

The feasibility of this approach depends on the type of database manager being used. Hierarchic and network databases, with their rich data structures, are well suited to storing the complex structures of composite objects. However, their inherent rigidity rules them out. Shutting down the database every time you modify a class would bring applications to a standstill!

*The relational model
is better but still
limited*

Relational databases suffer just the opposite problem; they offer the required flexibility, but their data structures are too simple to represent objects in their natural form. However, with enough disassembly and reassembly, it is possible to store objects in a relational database. Several research systems store objects in relational tables, and at least one commercial product now offers limited support for object storage.

Object Databases

A better solution to the problem of storing objects is to use a new kind of database, one that is designed to store and retrieve fully formed objects without reducing them to some arbitrary internal format. Databases of this type are known as **object database management systems (ODBMSs)**.

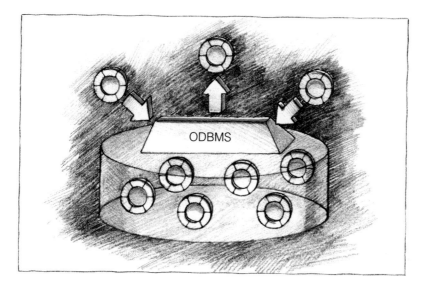

ODBMS

Object databases are built to hold objects

Object databases offer a better way to store objects because they provide all the traditional database services without the overhead of disassembling and reassembling objects every time they are stored and retrieved. Compared with an object database, storing complex objects in a relational database is tedious at best. It's like having to disassemble your car each night rather than just putting it into the garage!

Object databases solve the object storage problem

Storing Complex Information

Object databases offer both structure and flexibility

The major advantage of object databases over earlier types of databases is that they are able to represent complex information in a way that doesn't compromise flexibility. In effect, object databases represent the best of both worlds, combining the rich structure of the network models with the flexibility of the relational model. With object-oriented technology, it isn't necessary to give up one to get the other.

Support for Complex Structures

Composite objects support complex structures

In an object database, complex structures are represented by composite objects – that is, objects that contain other objects. These component objects can contain other objects in turn, and so on, allowing structures to be nested to any degree.

Composite objects actually contain references

Composite objects do not literally contain other objects, in the sense that one object is physically stored inside the other. Rather, composite objects contain *references* to other objects. In effect, composite objects contain the addresses of their component objects, allowing them to be accessed quickly when needed. Any given object can be "contained" in any number of composite objects simply by referring to it in each composite. As a result, the nested data structures of an object database can imitate the more general form of the network database model rather than being restricted to the hierarchic model.

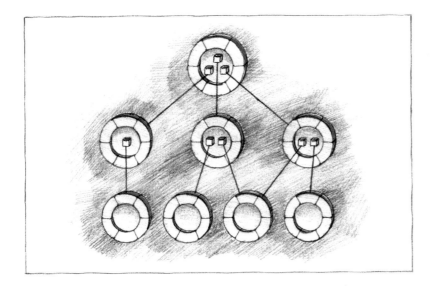

In fact, object databases can support any number of alternative structures for the same set of data. These alternative structures are not simply "views" of the data superimposed on a single underlying model, as in relational databases. All the structures are equally valid, and each one exists independently of all the others. You can create new structures and modify old ones without affecting other structures in any way. Again, object databases provide the rich structuring capabilities of network databases without suffering any of the rigidity that characterizes these systems.

*Object databases can
support multiple
structures*

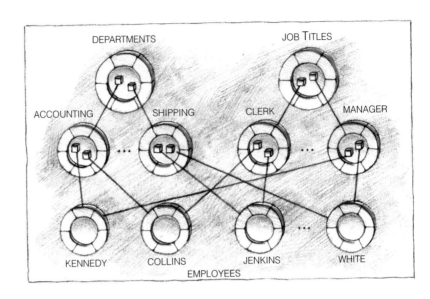

DEPARTMENTS

JOB TITLES

ACCOUNTING

SHIPPING

CLERK

MANAGER

KENNEDY

COLLINS

JENKINS

WHITE

EMPLOYEES

Abstraction in Object Databases

*Object databases
support new kinds
of information*

Like conventional databases, object databases typically include a set of
built-in data types to handle numbers, dates, dollar values, and other
common kinds of data. In the case of object databases, however, you can
extend these built-in types with new types to meet specialized needs, and
you can combine these new types to form still higher-level types, and so
on. In effect, you can customize an object database to hold any kind of
information you require. This customization can continue throughout
the life of the database.

*This data abstraction
elevates the thought
process*

This is another example of the power of data abstraction. Instead of being
constrained to think of your information in terms of how it is stored in
the machine, you can think of it in the terms you would normally use to
describe it. Object databases treat drawings as drawings, not as thousands
of related numbers and character sequences. Documents, departments,
transactions, and production lines can all be represented and viewed on
a similarly high level.

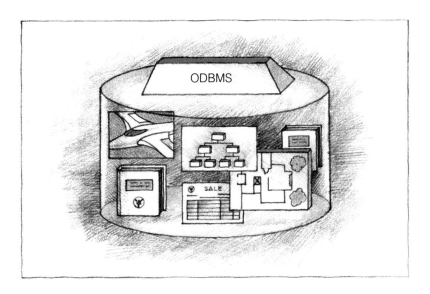

Because object databases can accommodate new data types, they are especially well suited to meet the increasing demand for multimedia information storage. Conventional databases were conceived and designed when computers dealt almost exclusively with text and numbers. Today, computers operate directly on a wide range of media, including drawings, blueprints, photographs, video sequences, human speech, sound patterns, and many other forms. An object database can easily store all these diverse kinds of information.

It also provides support for multimedia data

Flexibility Through Special Cases

The inheritance mechanism brings an additional level of flexibility to object databases. A common restriction imposed by conventional databases is that all entries of a given type must conform to the same structure. If new entries require a different structure, there are only two choices: force the new entries into the old structure, or define a new structure that includes the new requirements and convert all existing entries to fit it. Object databases offer a third choice: create a subclass to accommodate the exceptions, providing for the additional information without disturbing the existing entries.

Inheritance allows special cases

Here's an illustration to show why the third option is usually the best. Many non-U.S. addresses require an extra designator to record a township, county, parish, or the like. A company just beginning an overseas sales effort might find itself in the awkward situation of not being able to represent these addresses in its customer database. The company can't very well throw away the additional information. On the other hand, restructuring the database just to accommodate the new entries is not a cost-effective solution. In addition to the programming effort required to change both the database and the programs that access it, restructuring wastes valuable storage space for all the domestic customers, who don't use the added designator.

Creating a subclass solves the problem

An object database solves the problem by subclassing the customer address class. The new subclass simply defines an extra variable to hold the additional information, inheriting all its other characteristics from the regular address class. No changes are required to existing customers, and nothing is wasted because domestic customers aren't required to set aside space for information they don't use.

Special case of the address class

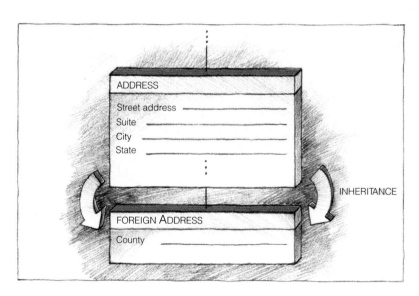

Retrieving Complex Data

Compared to relational databases, object databases can retrieve complex structures much more quickly because the structures are stored as direct references between objects. The object database doesn't have to reconstruct those relationships by searching through tables.

Object databases can be faster at retrieval

Consider how each type of database would represent the breakdown of a product into its component parts – something manufacturers call a **bill of materials** (**BOM**). A relational database would represent each product by a series of entries in a table which lists its components. Each of these components, in turn, would be defined by another series of entries, possibly in some other table. These subcomponents would be linked to still lower-level components, and so on, until the most elementary parts in the product were reached. A moderately complex product might require half a dozen levels of components with an average of, say, five components each for a total of over three thousand links. Each of these links would be formed by having a particular value – the part number in this case – appear in both entries.

Example: retrieving a bill of materials

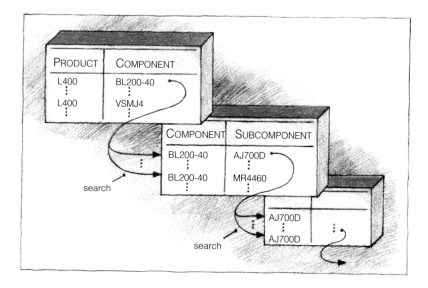

A BOM in a relational database

Retrieval based on searching is slow

Retrieving this bill of materials from a relational database can be a time-consuming process because the system must search the database each time it traces a link from one component to the next. If a component consists of parts BL200-40, VSMJ4, KS9000B, and MRG4400-D, then the database manager has to scan each of the appropriate tables to locate these part numbers. Relational databases have been optimized to perform this kind of search very quickly, but there is still a significant time penalty when thousands of searches are required to pull up a single structure.

References make retrieval fast and efficient

An object database stores a product as a composite object, with the links to its components represented as direct references. This representation eliminates the need to search through tables to find matching values because the database manager can go directly to the component objects. In the language of relational databases, all the required "joins" have been precomputed. In fact, you could retrieve the entire bill of materials with a single query to the database. The database would return the complete bill in a small fraction of the time required for a relational system.

A BOM in an object database

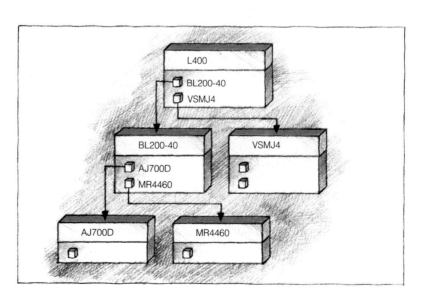

Building Intelligent Databases

Object databases can be divided into two broad categories – passive and active. Passive object databases store the structure of objects but do not implement their behavior, whereas active systems allow objects to execute and interact right in the database. The advantages of object databases described in the preceding sections apply to both types. The rest of the chapter examines the additional benefits of allowing objects to be active in the database.

Object databases can be passive or active

Passive and Active Object Databases

When a passive object database stores an object, it separates the object's methods from its data, usually placing the methods in an external file separate from the database. This means that you can't execute an object's methods while it's in the database. You have to remove the object from the database and place it in an application program before it can function again. In effect, a passive database keeps its objects in "cold storage" until they are taken out again.

Passive object databases store and retrieve structure

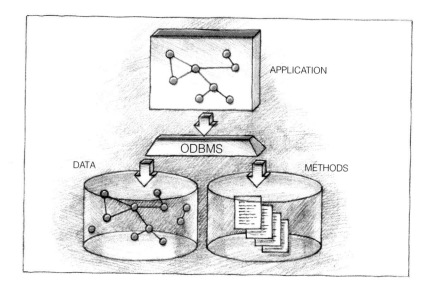

APPLICATION

ODBMS

DATA

METHODS

A passive object database

Passive object databases are fine for sharing objects

Passive object databases provide an excellent solution to the problem of storing and retrieving complex objects. For example, a designer using a computer-aided drawing (CAD) program could create engineering drawings out of complex objects, store those objects in the database, and then share them with other designers. A passive database is well suited to applications such as this because all it has to do is store and retrieve objects quickly and efficiently.

Active object databases provide a complete language

By contrast, active object databases store objects with "live" methods that can be activated directly in the database. This is no small accomplishment; active systems must include all the facilities of a complete programming language in order to execute methods in the database. But for applications that call for more than passive storage, the benefits are considerable. By supporting method execution, active databases bring the full power of object-oriented technology to bear on stored information.

An active object database

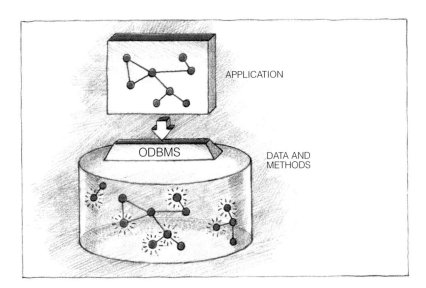

APPLICATION

ODBMS

DATA AND METHODS

Simplifying Database Access

Some of the most difficult problems in any data management system occur because multiple programs are allowed to share a common pool of data. The interaction that takes place through the shared data violates the principles of modular programming by creating dependencies among the programs. In fact, the problems that result when multiple programs access a shared database are virtually identical to the problems that arise when multiple subroutines share data within a single program. The only real difference is that in a database the problems occur on a much larger scale. Instead of being confined to a single program, they can affect the entire information structure of an organization!

Access to shared data causes problems

Here's a case in point. A typical corporate database may have several hundred application programs accessing the same collection of data. With a conventional database, every one of these programs must contain all the procedures to handle that information properly – to keep track of its data types and structure, to check incoming values for correct type and formatting, and so on.

Access routines must be included in every program

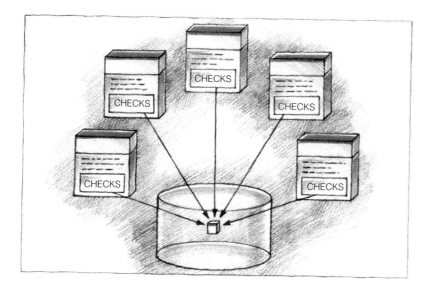

Redundant access routines

Redundant routines are very expensive

Duplicating these procedures in every program carries a number of hidden costs. First, all the programs are larger than they need to be and they take longer to write. Second, every time the procedures are duplicated the chances of creating a defective procedure increase. Finally, any change in a data structure requires every program to be revised, retested, and redeployed. This process can take many months and lead to any number of lingering errors.

Libraries of access routines aren't the solution

Many companies have tried to counter these problems by developing separate libraries of data access routines and requiring all programmers to use these routines. This approach has worked in some cases, but it doesn't solve all the problems. In fact, it can actually create some new ones. Programmers often have trouble locating the right access routines and wind up rewriting existing ones or just bypassing the library altogether. And any change to a data structure still requires that the access routines be changed, which in turn requires that all the application programs be rebuilt, and so on.

The solution is to let data manage its own access

The object-oriented solution puts the access routines right in the database, in the definitions of the data objects. This approach eliminates the duplicate procedures and makes all the programs shorter and easier to write. The likelihood of errors is significantly reduced because every program uses the same access routines. Changes to the data structures are also easier because you can hide most modifications within a single data object. As long as the programs still access the data through the same messages, none of them needs to be modified.

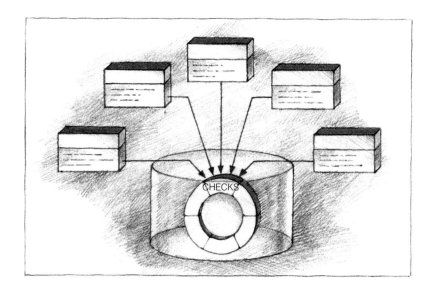

Self-Monitoring Data

In addition to handling data access, methods in object databases can
monitor the values of variables for special cases. Because ordinary data
is passive, it has no way to "speak up" when its value rises above or falls
below certain thresholds or takes on exceptional values. Any program
that depends on this data has to "poll" it periodically to check its value.
Polling is inefficient because it ties up computing resources while need-
lessly checking and rechecking data that hasn't changed.

Normally, data must be monitored through polling

Active objects, on the other hand, can monitor their own variables and
alert other objects about critical events. To add this self-awareness, you
simply include these checks in the methods that modify the variables.
This solution is not only more logical and compact, it's also more efficient
because values are checked only when they actually change.

Active objects can monitor their own variables

Built-in checks such as these are often called **triggers** because they alert the users of a system to exceptional situations. In a corporate database, well-placed triggers can constantly monitor the vital signs of the organization, providing readouts on demand and notifying the appropriate people if anything goes amiss. For example, inventory objects can automatically monitor their own stock and issue warnings if critical levels are reached. Similarly, an accounting system can include triggers for such key indicators as cash on hand and daily sales volume.

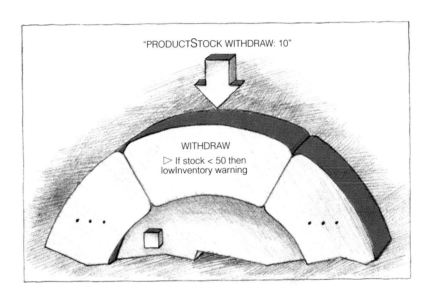

Object database triggers can be quite sophisticated

Most conventional databases now offer a simple form of triggering, but nothing on the scale of object databases. Because an active object database has the resources of a complete programming language, its triggers can be quite sophisticated. Active objects can perform computations, query other objects in the database, request information from users, and perform any number of checks and cross-checks before deciding whether a situation warrants special attention. On the output side, the result of a trigger can range from a simple on-screen notice to the preparation and distribution of a comprehensive analysis.

Applications in Object Databases

In fact, there's no limit to the complexity of the operations an active object database can carry out. If desired, entire applications can be embedded in the database. These applications enjoy a special advantage over applications that are isolated within separate programs. Applications in an object database are available to all the users of a system at all times, and not just when a particular user is running a particular program.

Applications can be embedded in object databases

Here's an example of an application that could benefit from being embedded in an object database. A number of programs on the market today manage the flow of electronic documents in an office, taking each document through a predefined sequence of operations and approvals. These programs don't perform the actual tasks of budgeting, editing, and so on. Rather, they monitor the current state of each document, recording its progress through channels, issuing reminders to people who should be acting on it, and otherwise shepherding it through its administrative life cycle.

Example: document management

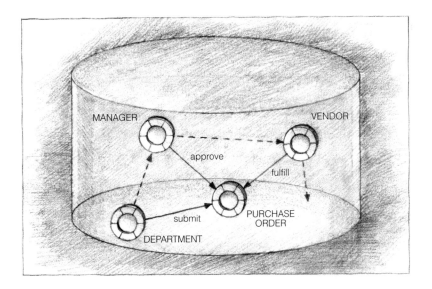

Document processing in an object database

This application is a natural for an object database

An active object database is a natural medium to support these tasks. While the checks and procedures involved are relatively simple, it's important that they be carried out immediately. An object database would trigger these activities automatically whenever a document was ready for the next step in its processing. Also, by encapsulating the appropriate procedures within each type of document, you would greatly simplify the task of creating and maintaining these procedures.

Intelligent Databases

Expertise may be expressed in an object's methods

The procedures built into this document-management system can express any amount of expertise about how documents are processed within the organization. If a document requires a signature from a manager who is on vacation, the system can execute a method to determine whether the resulting delay will pose a problem. If so, it could then identify someone else with the proper signature authority. In fact, the document object could engage in an extended reasoning process based on rules expressed in its methods.

This makes shared expert systems possible

Reasoning and problem solving are the established domain of **expert systems**. Expert systems are usually constructed as dedicated programs that operate on very restricted sets of data. In recent years, however, expert systems have begun to appear in broader applications, such as office automation, that call for shared information and problem solving. Increasingly, object databases are being viewed as the best medium for distributing that expertise. The basic technology underlying expert systems is very close to object-oriented technology – including the use of inheritance – so the mapping is a natural one.

The potential for building shared expert systems in active databases is exciting because it promises to bring a new dimension to corporate information systems. In the very near future, we will be able to build in rules and relationships that actually let our databases think for themselves, solving many administrative problems on the fly and recommending alternative approaches to handling others. The corporate database will no longer be a passive repository of data; it will become an active participant in the functioning of the organization.

Databases will soon become intelligent

The Role of Active Databases

Given their added capabilities, active object databases provide a broader spectrum of services than the passive variety. The passive type is ideal for storing and sharing complex objects, but it requires an object-oriented application program to activate its objects. By contrast, active databases can be used by any program, regardless of whether it is object-oriented. This means that active systems provide a much more general-purpose database. Because of their advantages, active object databases are beginning to play an important role in the creation of intelligent information systems.

Active object databases are general-purpose databases

7

Applying the Power of Objects

Clearly, object-oriented technology is not just another type of programming language, but something much more. In truth, this technology is nothing less than a grand attempt to redefine the entire process of software construction.

Object-oriented technology is more than a language

An Industrial Revolution for Software

A striking parallel exists between the methods of object-oriented technology and the transformation that took place in manufacturing during the Industrial Revolution. In the first section of this chapter, I explore this parallel to illustrate the potential rewards of the object-oriented approach to software development.

There's a parallel with the Industrial Revolution

Industry as Craft

Two hundred years ago, there was no manufacturing as we know it today. Products were created one at a time by highly trained craftsmen who learned their trade through long apprenticeship. Each craftsman was responsible for creating a complete product, and he enjoyed considerable latitude in the way he plied his trade. Each product bore the unique stamp of the man who made it, and each was, in a very real sense, a work of art.

Material goods used to be entirely hand crafted

A gunsmith, for example, created a rifle completely from scratch, starting with blocks of wood and pieces of iron. Each part was carefully fabricated to fit an individual weapon. Every screw was cut from rod stock, individually threaded, and hand fitted to the pieces it would fasten together. A finished rifle might have the same general design as other rifles in its class, but each one was unique in its details and performance.

Example: the fabrication of a rifle

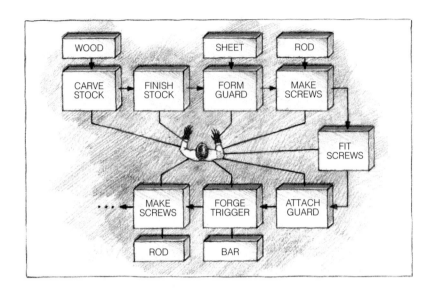

This is not an efficient approach to production

There is something aesthetically pleasing about this approach to the creation of material goods, and handcrafted products are often highly valued for their beauty and uniqueness. But the approach left much to be desired for an emerging industrial society. The process of individual crafting was painstakingly slow, the quality of the results varied with the skill of the craftsman, and the process was very expensive. Moreover, there was no way to standardize performance, and maintaining products in the field was often impossible because only the original craftsman could repair his creations.

A New Paradigm for Manufacturing

Eli Whitney developed a new approach

In 1798 inventor Eli Whitney conceived a new way of building rifles that led to the modern form of manufacturing. The central concept behind Whitney's approach was to assemble rifles out of standard parts that could be interchanged freely among the individual weapons. Specialists made each type of part, and rigorously defined standards ensured that these parts were functionally identical. Other specialists assembled the parts and tested the final product.

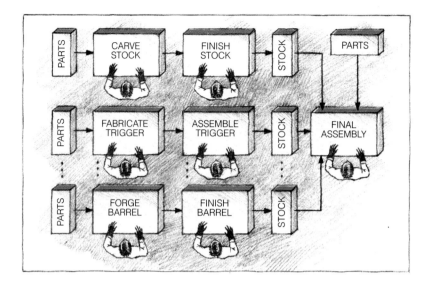

Whitney had to solve numerous technical problems before he could put his idea into practice, but the rewards outweighed the efforts. Rifles could be produced much faster, the overall quality was improved, and the cost of each weapon was greatly reduced. In addition, the weapons were not only more consistent in their performance, they were far easier to maintain because damaged rifles could be repaired with standard replacement parts.

This approach had many advantages

Whitney's approach was not a refinement of existing methods but a radical departure from an accepted way of thinking – what historians call a **paradigm shift**. A **paradigm** is a view of the world that is based on assumptions so ingrained that they are rarely questioned, such as the assumption that individual gunsmiths build complete weapons.

Whitney defined a new industrial paradigm

Paradigm shifts always come as a shock and take time to take hold, and the one Whitney precipitated was no exception. It took over fifty years for his method to spread to other industries, and the only reason it caught on as quickly as it did was the tremendous competitive advantage it gave to those who adopted it.

Paradigm shifts are always difficult transitions

A Paradigm Shift for Software

This is the way we build software today!

Two hundred years after the Industrial Revolution, the craft approach to producing material goods seems hopelessly antiquated. Yet this is precisely how we fabricate software systems today. Each program is a unique creation, constructed piece by piece out of the raw materials of a programming language by skilled software craftspeople. Each component of the program is fabricated specifically for the role it will play in its particular program and can rarely be used in the construction of other programs.

The results are typical of craft production

Conventional programming is roughly on a par with manufacturing two hundred years ago. Programs are expensive and time-consuming to build, and their quality is highly dependent on the skills of the craftspeople involved. Because each program is unique, standardization is very difficult and maintenance is a major challenge for anyone other than the original makers of the program.

The goal is an Industrial Revolution for software

This comparison with the Industrial Revolution reveals the true ambition behind the object-oriented approach. The goal is not just to improve the programming process but to define an entirely new paradigm for software construction. Like all paradigm shifts, this one will meet with resistance and skepticism, but it will prevail if it delivers its promised benefits. And if it does succeed, the object-oriented paradigm will bring about a true revolution for the computer age.

The Value of Reusable Components

Reusable objects are essential

Success for the object-oriented approach depends on the development of standard, reusable objects comparable to Whitney's interchangeable rifle parts. These objects will be the fundamental building blocks of future software.

Designing for Reuse

In a way, the standardization problem is much easier to solve in software because the actual production of components is trivial. Once you define a class, all instances of that class are guaranteed to be identical and perfectly formed. Objects can be produced in any quantity, they are available immediately, and there are no manufacturing costs. It's a manufacturer's dream!

Reliable production of objects is not the problem

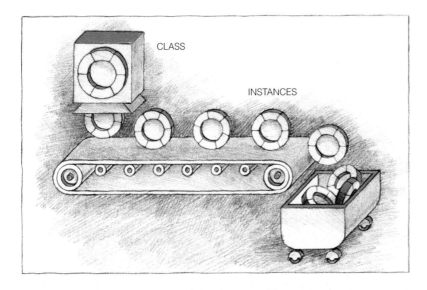

A class 'manufacturing' instances

The challenge of applying Whitney's method to software construction, then, is not on the production side but on the engineering side. Designers of object-oriented systems must define classes so they are universally applicable and easily reusable.

The challenge lies in getting the classes right

This is not an easy task. To create a reusable class, you must take a much broader perspective than normal software development requires. While the immediate uses of a class may be obvious, future uses can be difficult to foresee. What other services will the class need to support these new uses? What features have crept into its present form that are unique to the current application and will become baggage in future uses?

Reusability takes planning and effort

Classes must be allowed to evolve

The trick is to make a class complete enough to satisfy all the expected needs, while also keeping it simple and independent of other classes to maintain good modularity. The perfect design is rarely achieved on the first pass, which adds another constraint on the design of classes. They must be constructed in an open-ended way so that they can evolve to meet new needs while still satisfying the original set of requirements.

There are three basic sources of classes

Fortunately, the burden of creating good, reusable classes does not fall entirely on the developers of object-oriented applications. There are actually three major sources for obtaining reusable classes: some come with the various object-oriented programming languages, others are supplied by software companies that specialize in building reusable classes, and the remainder are constructed by developers in house.

Three sources of classes

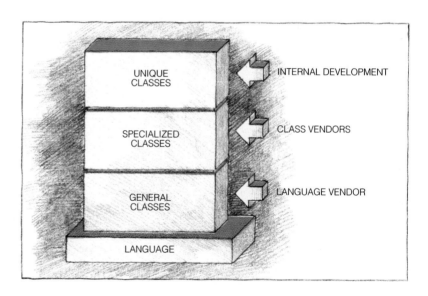

Classes That Come with Object-Oriented Languages

Smalltalk is a good example of an object-oriented language that provides a comprehensive library of reusable classes. Smalltalk's built-in classes handle everything from simple addition to complex display management. C++, by contrast, doesn't include any built-in classes as part of its basic definition. However, publishers of C++ systems usually supply a basic set of classes with their products to help programmers get started, and some vendors provide extensive class libraries.

Languages vary in their class offerings

Whatever the language, the supplied classes tend to be very general so they can fit the needs of almost any application. Some typical services provided by these classes are maintaining collections of objects, placing windows on the screen, and defining abstract data types.

Included classes tend to be general purpose

Buying from Class Vendors

We are witnessing the beginning of a new industry – companies whose primary business is building and selling reusable classes. Only a handful of these companies exist today, but their number should grow rapidly as the demand for classes increases. As a rule, class vendors offer more specialized sets of classes than the ones supplied with object-oriented languages. For example, one vendor supplies classes for scientific applications, and another sells classes for graphic displays.

Software publishers now sell specialized classes

Like the classes that come with object-oriented languages, vendor-supplied classes are invariably language-specific. So a company using Smalltalk must buy Smalltalk classes. Unfortunately, there's no simple way to convert classes from one language to another.

These classes are language-specific

Because the industry is still quite young, classes from independent class vendors tend to vary greatly in style and quality. Also, classes from different vendors are often incompatible with each other even if they're written for the same language. As the industry matures, emerging standards should allow class packages to be mixed and matched more freely.

Commercial classes vary in quality and rarely mix

Building Your Own Classes

Classes may also be built in house

To supplement the classes supplied with object-oriented languages and by outside vendors, companies can develop their own custom classes. At present, object-oriented development groups are pursuing this option for most of their classes. However, this pattern is bound to change as standard, proven classes become more widely available. Given the difficulty of building high-quality, general-purpose classes, it's hardly economical for companies to reinvent low-level classes when they should be concentrating on high-level assemblies. That would make about as much sense as building contractors forging their own nails!

The most specialized classes should be custom built

In general, development teams should focus on building the specialized classes that are unique to a company's line of business or operating procedures. These are the classes that are least likely to exist on the open market, and they are also the ones most likely to provide a competitive advantage to the company that builds them.

A New Approach to Software Construction

Objects must be assembled into solutions

Building up the right inventory of reusable objects is the first step in creating object-oriented software systems. The obvious next step would be to assemble these objects into working solutions. However, it turns out that there is an alternative to going directly from reusable objects to complete solutions. This intermediate step complicates matters in the short term but greatly simplifies them in the long run.

Building Solutions Directly on Objects

Solutions can be built directly on base objects

The conventional approach to software development is to define a problem, devise a solution to it, and then translate the solution into procedures. This approach works fine with objects, and many development teams use object technology in just this way, especially in their early projects. But this approach sacrifices a great deal of the object-oriented advantage by limiting reusability to the most basic level of objects.

To see why, consider what it means to assemble objects into a solution. An object-oriented program consists entirely of objects interacting through messages. The only way you can get existing objects to do anything different is by defining high-level control objects that send them new combinations of messages. So, when you assemble existing objects into solutions, you're really defining new classes of objects and setting them into action.

Objects are assembled by adding new classes

New classes define solutions

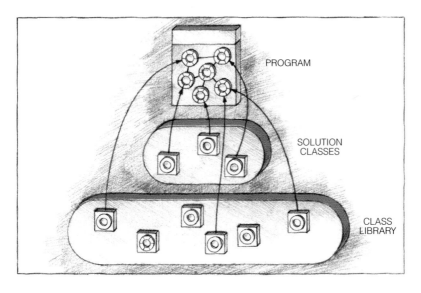

You could base these high-level objects purely on the needs of a particular problem, as the conventional approach would call for. But in that case you would have to create new high-level objects from scratch for each a new problem. There's a better way to build up solutions, and it stems from the original purpose of object-oriented languages – simulation.

Adding objects for specific solutions is limiting

The Power of Modeling

The way to get the most out of object-oriented technology is to construct a working model of some aspect of your company's operations, building up the model to higher and higher levels until a handful of additional objects can get it to do something new and interesting. Only then does the effort shift to solving specific problems.

A better approach is to build a working model

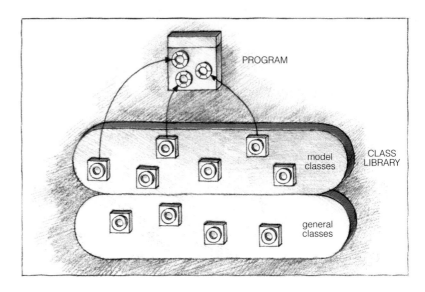

*This approach has
important advantages*

This model-building strategy has some important advantages. All the
higher-level objects, as well as the model itself, are general purpose in
nature and can be reused in future projects. In addition, solutions built
on the model are more flexible than solutions based directly on low-
level objects. If your company's operations change, you can usually
change the underlying model without making any changes whatever
to the high-level classes that implement specific solutions!

*There are costs to
modeling that must
be amortized*

Of course, these benefits come at a price; it takes more time, energy, and
foresight to construct a general model than it does to craft specialized solutions. To justify these costs, you must amortize them over multiple development projects. It's only after the model has been used to solve several
different problems that the investment in building the model pays off in
faster development and more adaptable solutions.

*Example: extending
a billing program*

To illustrate this payoff, consider the example from Chapter 2 in which
a billing system is asked to handle customer mailings and sales ticklers.
In a conventional system, this request is unreasonable in the extreme.
The billing system was constructed for a very specific purpose, and it
would require major reconstruction to handle these added functions.

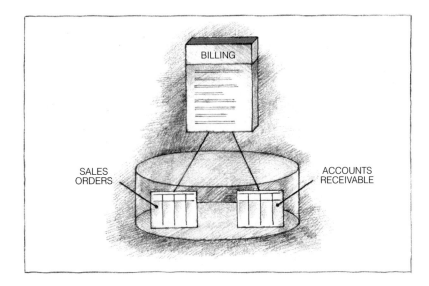

BILLING

SALES
ORDERS

ACCOUNTS
RECEIVABLE

By contrast, a general-purpose model of a company's interactions with its customers could handle all three applications and more. To solve the billing problem, the model would necessarily include classes for representing communications to and from customers, such as orders, shipments, bills, and payments. To extend the model, you would simply add the new classes for mailings and ticklers. All the tracking and reporting services for communications would automatically apply to these new communication types without any fundamental changes to the model.

A model of customer interactions is more flexible

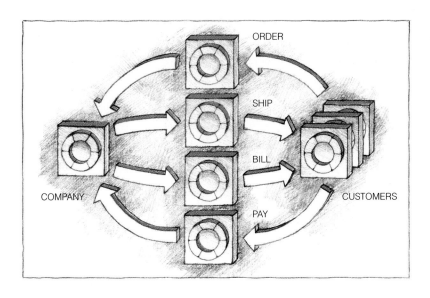

ORDER

SHIP

BILL

COMPANY

PAY

CUSTOMERS

Rapid Prototyping

*Modeling makes rapid
development possible*

Of course, reusable objects and operational models must be translated into solutions at *some* point. But by the time a company is ready to solve a particular problem, the additional work required to implement a solution on top of an existing model is only a small fraction of the effort that would be required to build up the solution from scratch. Being a much smaller step, it can be taken more directly, using a technique known as rapid prototyping.

*Rapid prototyping
demonstrates a
solution quickly*

With **rapid prototyping**, a manager provides an informal description of the problem to be solved, such as adding mailings to a customer management system. A programmer starts with the existing model of customer interactions and, drawing on standard objects for creating form letters, menu interfaces, and activity reports, pulls together a rough prototype of a system. Given the rapid nature of object assembly, an experienced programmer can usually have something up and running within a few days, or at most a couple of weeks.

At that point, the manager and programmer sit down together with the prototype and evaluate it. The two continue to work as partners, refining both the problem and its solution until the prototype is far enough along to put into daily use. Unlike conventional prototypes, the object-oriented prototype is never thrown away. Through the flexibility of object-oriented software, the programmer can gradually transform the prototype from an initial sketch into a production program. And this program continues to evolve even after it's put into service, acquiring new features and adapting to the changing needs of the business.

The solution emerges from a partnership

Rapid prototyping

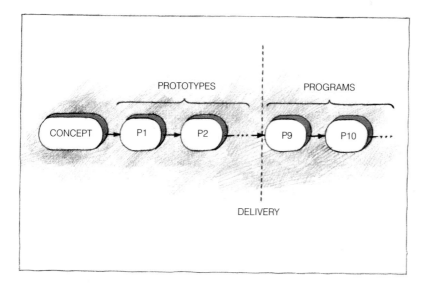

This approach to software development is much faster than the conventional "waterfall" methodology practiced in most large companies today, which requires the creation and approval of numerous detailed documents before the first procedure is ever written. The object-oriented approach also results in better systems because the conventional methodology doesn't allow any modifications once the actual programming has begun. This constraint frustrates managers to no end because they rarely know what they really want until they see it running on a screen, at which point it's too late to make any changes!

This approach is fast and produces better systems

**The conventional
development cycle**

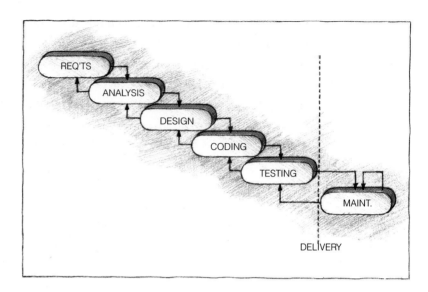

*The structure of
the waterfall is just
an illusion*

Despite its advantages, rapid prototyping has met with strong resistance
from information systems professionals because it's so unstructured compared to the conventional approach. However, the structure of the waterfall methodology is more apparent than real. Studies of actual practice
have shown that software development rarely follows the rigorously
defined steps of the conventional model. Companies quite commonly
redefine projects to meet changing needs even as the final procedures
are being written and tested!

*This is frustrating
but unavoidable*

This subversion of the conventional software development cycle frustrates
everyone involved. However, the reality of software development today
is that things don't stay stable long enough in the business world to allow
the luxury of such a drawn-out, multistage process – even if it were the
ideal way to develop systems. Rapid prototyping is a much more realistic
response to the increasing demand for rapid software development.

Rapid prototyping should not, however, be confused with the ad hoc, un-structured programming style known as "hacking." Rapid prototyping in object-oriented development is highly structured because new solutions are constructed out of proven, standard objects already working within a consistent model of a company's operations. Object-oriented prototyping is not an excuse to abandon all discipline in software construction. Rather, it's simply a different, faster way of producing disciplined, well-structured programs.

But rapid prototyping is not the same as "hacking"

Evolutionary Systems

This, then, is the general sequence for constructing object-oriented systems: build up a library of reusable classes, use those classes to construct models of corporate processes, and overlay solutions on these models through rapid prototyping. These three stages of development interact considerably as each stage provides feedback to the earlier stages – solving new problems reveals shortcomings in the model, spurring the development of new classes, and so on.

Object-oriented systems are built in three stages

Three layers of construction

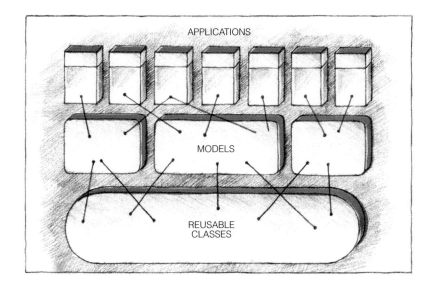

Systems may be delivered many times

These three stages are not, however, the entirety of object-oriented development. Unlike conventional software, object-oriented programs are built to be changed. Object-oriented systems are "delivered" many times during the prototyping phase, and they continue to be refined and re-delivered as they evolve in the future. Unlike conventional prototyping, object-oriented prototypes are never thrown away and replaced with "production" versions, so the only real difference between the prototype and production phases is that the system is actually placed in use.

There is a danger in this approach

Of course, there is a problem lurking in this approach to software development; if systems are never formally "done," then it can be very difficult to control the time and costs of developing them. In fact, object-oriented systems are especially vulnerable to the "creeping feature creature" because it's so easy to add features to a working prototype.

Explicit phases and deadlines are required

The most effective solution to this problem is to set a budget and deadline for the development of a basic set of functionality, with a "wish list" of desirable additions. The prototyping effort consists of implementing the basic features and then rolling in as many extras as will fit within the time and dollar constraints. Once the cutoff point is reached, functionality is frozen and the effort is focused on transforming the prototype into a robust deployable system. Further additions are planned and budgeted as distinct phases of development.

Object-oriented systems grow and develop

The evolutionary nature of object-oriented development is often compared to organic or social growth. Complex, large-scale systems are rarely designed in the abstract and then assembled according to a fixed blueprint. Certainly such human constructions as skyscrapers and jet aircraft are explicitly designed. But even these complex systems pale beside the scale and sophistication of such natural systems as a planetary ecology or even a single human body, systems which evolved over millennia of variation and selection. Similarly, such complex cultural artifacts as law, government, and free enterprise are all products of cultural trial and error.

These parallels suggest that the object-oriented approach to software development, with its emphasis on growth and adaptation, may be able to produce far more sophisticated systems than conventional techniques of analysis and design. If so, this new technology will strike to the very heart of the software crisis, allowing us to develop far larger systems than we can presently conceive and design.

This may permit far more sophisticated systems

8

Evaluating the Risks and Benefits

Before managers can make informed decisions about adopting a new technology, the advantages of this technology must be translated into measurable benefits. Equally important, the disadvantages of the technology must also be assessed. This chapter offers a candid summary of the potential costs and benefits of object-oriented technology.

This is a candid cost-benefit analysis

In the interest of brevity and balance, I've boiled the analysis down to seven arguments for and seven against adopting the technology. The chapter concludes with some counsel on how a company can explore the technology further and make its own assessment of the costs and benefits.

Here are seven arguments for and against

Potential Benefits

Object-oriented software construction promises many of the same benefits as modern manufacturing: faster production, higher quality, and easier maintenance, all at reduced cost. The object-oriented approach should also lead to larger-scale systems that organize information more effectively and adapt more easily to changing needs.

The benefits are comparable to manufacturing

1. Faster Development

One obvious advantage of the object-oriented approach is that you can produce finished software in a fraction of the time required with conventional methods. This time savings is actually the result of three separate techniques: building software out of standard objects, reusing existing models of corporate processes, and replacing conventional development phases with rapid prototyping.

Development is faster for three reasons

The faster develop-
ment comes from
what isn't done

Notice that I'm not suggesting that it's faster to write object-oriented programs on a line-by-line basis; in fact, it's often slower. The speed advantage comes entirely from the work that *isn't* done to create a new program – all the programming effort that is reused from existing objects, all the design work that went into an existing model of a process, and all the formal procedures that are bypassed by rapid prototyping. Simply switching to an object-oriented language won't accelerate the development process at all. The entire methodology must be followed in order to realize significant reductions in development time.

Many proponents of object technology claim a tenfold improvement in development time using object-oriented techniques over conventional programming methods. Unfortunately, no one has published a controlled, side-by-side comparison of the two approaches to provide solid evidence for this claim. However, there is a growing body of anecdotal evidence to support productivity improvements of at least five-to-one, and many report much higher gains. The most tightly controlled comparison I'm aware of resulted in a fourteen-to-one improvement in productivity for a mainstream business application, so there is little doubt that major reductions in development time can be realized.

2. Higher Quality

There are several
sources of quality
enhancement

Object-oriented technology can not only speed development, it can also improve quality. This increase in quality stems mostly from the fact that programs are assembled out of existing, proven components rather than being written from scratch every time. In addition, the superior modularization of object technology reduces the interactions among the components of a program, making it easier to verify that the program functions correctly under all possible circumstances.

Of course, object-oriented technology does not, in itself, guarantee improvements in quality. In fact, it's just as easy to write bad object-oriented programs as it is to write bad programs using conventional techniques. What object-oriented technology offers is a new set of tools for building quality into software. The commitment to quality must come from the companies and individuals who use that technology.

Quality must always be instilled by people

3. Easier Maintenance

Object-oriented technology can also ease the burden of software maintenance, particularly the detection and repair of defects. Of course, the best maintenance program is to build quality into a product in the first place. Object-oriented technology can reduce maintenance requirements simply because it produces higher quality systems. Assuming that defects do surface in an object-oriented system, you can usually locate them easily because of the natural mapping between the structure of the software and the real-world system it models.

Maintenance is easier in object-oriented programs

Once defects are located, repairs are typically easier to implement because the modularity of object-oriented software allows changes to be constrained to a small part of the program. A common problem in repairing conventional programs is that each repair creates two new defects, each of which has to be located and repaired, creating four new defects, and so on. This kind of chain reaction is much less likely in an object-oriented system because the effects of changes are more localized.

Repairs are easier to make

4. Reduced Cost

Object-oriented technology reduces software development costs in three areas: programming, system design, and administration. The programming effort is lessened because you can assemble new programs out of existing components. Rapid prototyping reduces the design and administrative aspects of software development, which often account for as much as eighty percent of the total effort. These reduced resource demands translate directly into cost savings.

Faster development requires fewer resources

Buying components is cheaper than making them	As commercial collections of reusable classes become increasingly available, companies will be able to save money by buying standard classes rather than building them in house. Because class vendors can amortize their costs over many sales, they can sell reusable classes for a small fraction of what it costs to develop them. This will offer companies an attractive alternative to the classic make/buy decision; they can buy standard components from commercial vendors and do only the final assembly in house. The result is a custom program developed for a fraction of the usual cost.
Reducing maintenance also reduces cost	Higher-quality systems and reduced maintenance requirements also result in cost savings. Since maintenance often accounts for more than half the total cost of a system, companies can save a substantial amount in that area.

5. Increased Scalability

Object-oriented technology scales better	Given its improved modularization, object-oriented programming is especially well suited to developing large-scale systems. Large systems are easier to build and maintain when you build them out of subsystems that can be developed and tested independently. In addition, by using the overloading techniques described in Chapter 4, you can add new types of objects to a system without modifying the existing objects. This allows you to grow a system organically rather than redesign it with each expansion. In short, object-oriented technology combines the power of modular programming with the advantages of polymorphism to allow systems to scale up more gracefully than ever before.
Extensibility requires careful planning	Support for large-scale systems is one of the most important potential benefits of object-oriented technology. However, object-oriented programming does not automatically make large systems feasible. Experience to date suggests that graceful scaling occurs only for systems that are built on solid, general-purpose classes and that make use of accurate, flexible models.

6. Better Information Structures

Through the use of composite objects, class hierarchies, and other structures, object-oriented technology can effectively represent the increasingly complex information businesses now rely on. Moreover, this increased complexity does not come at the cost of accessibility. The fact that object-oriented structures reflect the way people naturally organize and understand the real world means that the richer structures make information more accessible, not less.

Information structures are more sophisticated

A related benefit is that by packaging procedures with data, information systems can go beyond the representation of structure to include actions as well. This represents a transition from information systems to *knowledge systems,* which not only organize the information of a business but also initiate appropriate actions in response to that information.

They can also include action components

7. Increased Adaptability

No matter how perfectly crafted, a program is useless if it doesn't meet current needs. Unfortunately for traditional development methods, the needs of modern organizations are changing at an ever-increasing rate. The adaptability of object-oriented programs may well turn out to be the most crucial advantage of object-oriented technology.

Adaptability is essential

With object-oriented software, you can make local changes in a program without rebuilding the entire system. For example, you can add new kinds of objects that were never part of the original design – new kinds of products, say, or interfaces to new machines – and all the other objects in the system will treat them as though they had been there from the beginning. This is one of the key advantages offered by message-based programming.

Changes can be made without rebuilding a system

Potential Concerns

There are valid concerns about the technology

While object-oriented technology promises many benefits, there are some valid concerns about its ability to deliver those benefits. Most of these concerns have to do with temporary limitations and should disappear as the technology and its market mature. However, they remain important considerations for anyone evaluating the technology at the present time.

1. Maturity of the Technology

The technology is still evolving

Even though it's been around for over twenty years, object-oriented programming is not yet a stable technology. Most of those two decades were spent in research labs, where the emphasis is on innovation rather than commercialization. In the long run this research will improve the technology. But this academic emphasis creates some concerns for companies seeking to deploy the technology today.

Software may have to be modified for new features

One problem is that working systems may need to be modified in order to take advantage of new developments in the technology. This will probably not be a major problem, because new versions of object-oriented languages are now designed to support systems that were developed with earlier versions, making modifications optional rather than required. But it is a consideration.

There are no proven development methodologies

More importantly, developing object-oriented systems is still more of an art than a science. While some of the basic principles are clear – build for reusability, model real-world systems, and maximize modularity, to name three – the actual techniques and procedures for applying these principles are not well established. A body of rules comparable to structured programming will be required to provide guidance and discipline to object-oriented development efforts.

2. Need for Standards

Because the technology is still evolving, it lacks well-established standards to enforce consistency among different implementations of a particular language. Without accepted standards, companies may have difficulty moving programs from one development environment to another. This lack of portability raises concerns about relying on a single vendor for critical information systems. If the vendor goes out of business, what happens to the systems?

There are no accepted standards for languages

The lack of accepted standards also makes it difficult to mix and match classes from different vendors when building up a library of reusable classes. This is not yet a major problem only because there are so few vendors of reusable classes. But it will become a serious concern in the next few years as companies begin to rely on outside suppliers for the basic building blocks of their information systems.

It's hard to mix classes from different vendors

3. Need for Better Tools

There is also a shortage of good tools for supporting object-oriented development efforts. These tools include programs to assist in the design of objects, manage libraries of reusable objects, design and maintain data-input forms and reports, and coordinate the development efforts of large teams of programmers.

There is a shortage of appropriate software tools

Tools to facilitate the use of new technologies always lag behind the introduction of those technologies, and object-oriented technology is no exception. But the problem may be more acute in this case because the object-oriented approach is so different from its predecessors.

Tools always lag behind technology

The problem of managing class libraries is a case in point. An object-oriented development team spends most of its time reusing existing classes, and most of *that* time is spent selecting the appropriate class out of the hundreds or even thousands available in the library. Given the amount of time programmers spend in this activity, it's important to have good tools for locating classes based on their category, purpose, origin, usage, and other key characteristics. At best, contemporary object-oriented languages provide simple "browsers" that allow searching for classes based on one or two of these qualities.

4. Speed of Execution

Because they provide more services than conventional languages, object-oriented languages may produce software that executes more slowly than conventional programs. For example, a program may have to compare the number and data types of the parameters in a message to determine which method to invoke. The convenience of reusing names may cost you some execution speed.

Actually, concerns about the speed of object-oriented systems are largely based on early research systems that were not designed for speed. Modern object-oriented languages have been highly optimized for performance and are nearly as fast as conventional languages.

And they can be
faster with complex
information

Although the added power of object-oriented programming may extract a small speed penalty, it can also increase speed in many circumstances. The most dramatic increase comes when programs work with complex information stored in databases. When the information is stored in the relational form of tables tied together by cross references, storing and retrieving complex structures can be a time-consuming process. Storing these structures directly as composite objects allows them to be accessed in a fraction of the time.

5. Availability of Qualified Personnel

Another problem for object-oriented technology is that few people in the commercial arena really understand how to use it effectively. The most obvious aspect of this problem is a shortage of experienced object-oriented programmers, but the problem runs deeper than this.

There is a shortage of object-oriented programmers

Because the technology requires an entirely different approach to software development, project managers and executives alike must understand the nature of object-oriented development. Without this understanding, companies are likely to adopt object-oriented technology without making the required investment in reusable classes and models or converting to rapid prototyping. In this event, the technology will disappoint them no matter how good their programmers are.

Managers must also be qualified in the technology

The shortage of qualified personnel can be addressed through hiring, training, or a combination of the two. In the case of training, however, something more than the usual programming courses is required. The conversion to object-oriented technology requires an education in new concepts and principles. This education must include everyone who is involved in the design and construction of new systems.

Converting requires education as well as training

6. Costs of Conversion

There are significant costs associated with making the transition to object-oriented technology. The most obvious cost is the investment in new software; companies must acquire new languages, databases, and tools to make use of the technology. However, object-oriented languages and tools are priced comparably to conventional development systems. A larger cost may come in the form of new hardware. Because most object-oriented systems make extensive use of graphics, companies that rely primarily on character-based terminals accessing mainframe computers may need to invest in some workstation-class machines or personal computers.

Software and hardware purchases may be required

There's a learning curve to get up to speed

Education and training for managers and technical staff can also be costly. In addition, programmers can experience a loss of productivity as they learn to work effectively with the new concepts and techniques. Experience to date suggests that while programmers can begin writing object-oriented programs within a few weeks, full productivity in the new techniques may require six months or more of active use.

There's also an investment in classes and models

Another cost of converting to the object-oriented approach – one which is often neglected – is the expense of building up a library of reusable classes and developing reusable models of corporate processes. This is actually the biggest cost of conversion, but it's also the one with the greatest payoff in the long run because it provides a platform for the rapid deployment of new systems. It also contains a hidden benefit that may be appreciated only in retrospect: the process of building up reusable classes and models requires a thorough examination of the components and operations of a company. This analysis is bound to produce new insights into the business and may well result in significant improvements.

7. Support for Large-Scale Modularity

Modularity is limited to the local level

The packaging of methods and data within objects provides unprecedented support for modularity at a fine-grain level. Unfortunately, object-oriented technology offers only limited support for combining groups of objects into larger functional modules. Composite objects offer the best mechanism for building larger modules, but they fail to hide their internals the way simple objects do. External objects can directly access the objects contained within a composite object, violating one of the essential principles of modularization.

Programmers can compensate for the lack of explicit, high-level modules by agreeing not to access the internals of composite objects directly. However, failure to adhere to this discipline can lead to the object-oriented equivalent of what used to be known as "spaghetti code" back before the advent of structured programming. This term refers to complex patterns of leaps and loops that snake through a program and are nearly impossible for anyone but the original programmer to follow. In the case of object-oriented programs, the corresponding problem takes the form of what might be called "ravioli code" – lots of tiny, well structured objects that are easy to understand in isolation, but whose interactions are nearly impossible to decipher.

Lack of structure can lead to "ravioli code"

In the Balance

The promise of object-oriented technology is great, but the concerns listed above cannot be ignored. Fortunately, the current push to commercialize the technology is causing many changes which address these concerns.

The technology is maturing rapidly

Signs of Maturation

Standards for object-oriented systems are on the way. Official standards organizations are now working to define standards for Smalltalk, C++, and other object-oriented languages. In addition, the major vendors of object-oriented products have formed a consortium, the **Object Management Group** (**OMG**), to promote the adoption of standards and the interchangeability of objects and classes. Throughout the industry, companies are making a concerted effort to bring the various languages, tools, class libraries, and databases together into complete, working solutions.

The technology is stabilizing and standardizing

Now that languages are beginning to stabilize, vendors are starting to compete on the basis of their tools. This competition is producing better tools and increasingly sophisticated development environments. There is also a push to develop analysis and design methods suitable for object-oriented development. A few companies now provide CASE products that automate these new methods.

Tools are improving rapidly

The costs of adoption are falling

The shortage of qualified personnel is being addressed by a wide variety of courses in both universities and private training companies. In addition, the costs of conversion are dropping as competition makes a wider range of products available at lower prices. Although well-designed reusable classes are still in short supply, more choices will become available as more companies adopt the technology and create increased demand.

Deciding Whether to Give It a Try

There are risks to both action and inaction

The first decision a company has to make with regard to object-oriented technology is whether or not to give it a try. Given the drawbacks, there are clearly risks associated with getting into the technology too soon. But there are risks associated with waiting as well. If the technology really pays off on its promise, the companies that begin the transition now will enjoy an important competitive advantage while the others strive to catch up with them.

A prudent strategy is to run a pilot project

Probably the most prudent strategy is to avoid the extremes of ignoring the technology or committing vital systems to it. Instead, companies can make a modest investment in a pilot program to gain first-hand experience with object-oriented development. This approach allows a company to reach its own conclusions about the value of the technology, and it places the company well down the experience curve if it converts to object-oriented development in the future.

Running a Pilot Project

Don't use traditional development procedures

If you decide to undertake a pilot project within your own company, it's important to avoid running it like a typical software project. If you follow the usual procedure of setting up a team, picking a problem, and programming a solution from scratch, the experiment will almost certainly fail. Not only will the learning curve offset any possible advantages, the project will include all the overhead of conversion with very few of the benefits.

The only way to really evaluate the object-oriented approach is to apply the methodology fully. Pick an area of operations and build a working model of it, building up a small library of reusable classes in the process. Then use this model to solve a series of application problems in succession, using rapid prototyping in place of the conventional software development cycle. By the time you finish the third application, the benefits of the object-oriented approach should be fully evident.

Evaluate the full object-oriented methodology

If you want to measure the benefits of object-oriented technology before going beyond the pilot stage, you'll need to conduct a side-by-side comparison with conventional development methods. Few companies have done this to date, but it's really a small investment in view of the potential costs and benefits of adopting the technology.

A controlled comparison will measure benefits

A simple way to conduct the experiment is to have a separate group of programmers tackle the third application problem using conventional design and programming methods. To avoid confounding the experiment with heroic efforts, make sure that neither group knows that a controlled experiment is in progress. When both systems are done, have an unbiased observer compare them in terms of program size, execution speed, resource requirements, time to completion, number of defects, and overall quality. These comparisons should provide ample quantitative evidence for the benefits of the object-oriented methodology.

Have a second group build the same application

For a really thorough test, prepare a list of modifications to the finished application and see how easily each of the two teams can adapt its solutions to the new requirements. Treat the modifications as a second development project, and collect all the same information as before. In terms of a cost/benefit analysis, this second set of measures is even more important than the first because the costs of modifications to software usually exceed the original development costs.

Ask both groups to perform modifications

The Bottom Line

The benefits appear to outweigh the costs

If you compare the costs and benefits, the balance is clearly in favor of the object-oriented approach. Object-oriented technology appears to offer a fundamentally better way to construct software, and it shows real promise for resolving the software crisis.

But only you can decide

But this superiority is not yet an accepted conclusion. For anyone who has witnessed the rise and fall of "cure-all" technologies in the past, it's hard to take any of these claims on faith. The real bottom line is this: because the object-oriented approach has so much potential, any company with its own software development organization ought to explore this new methodology and check out the benefits for itself. As more and more companies do this, the superiority of object-oriented technology will quickly leave the realm of promises and become an established fact.

9

The Future of Software

Object-oriented technology has already changed the way we *build* software, and it's beginning to change the way we *design* our software as well. Soon it will change the very *nature* of software into something we would barely recognize today. Here are some of the changes to look for.

The very nature of software is changing

Mix-and-Match Software

As object-oriented technology becomes more widely adopted, the definition of a program will change dramatically. With the exception of some mainframe packages, programs are usually delivered as "closed systems." All the ingredients of the program are created by its developers and are locked into a final form before the program is shipped. Although the buyers of the program may have some configuration options, they are explicitly barred from physically modifying the program and adapting it to their needs.

Programs are usually closed systems

Object-oriented technology could completely reverse this situation. Under the right conditions, objects can be linked together at any time, even while a program is running. Given this facility, it's possible to deliver working programs in parts. The various parts don't have to be purchased at the same time, or even from the same vendor. As long as the parts are all compatible and provide the required services, customers can assemble them in whatever configuration suits their unique needs.

Object technology makes open systems possible

This is comparable to open hardware systems

This breakthrough in software configuration could have the same liberating effect as open systems had on hardware. Nowadays, virtually all computers allow you to plug specialized circuit boards into internal slots. You can mix and match such hardware options as displays, printers, scanners, and network interfaces, selecting each device on the basis of its features, vendor, and price.

Open systems are complicated but flexible

Because all the components must work in every possible combination, the open-systems approach to hardware has complicated life for everyone involved, from manufacturers to distributors to consumers. But the resulting adaptability has more than justified the complications. Despite many complaints, computer purchasers have shown an overwhelming preference for open systems.

The same tradeoff will occur in software

Object-oriented technology promises to bring the same openness to software, along with the same complications and benefits. Suppose, for example, that user interfaces were separate from the programs that used them. You could invest in a single interface with the look and feel you prefer, and all your programs would automatically use that interface. Similarly, you could buy separate hardware interfaces to control the specific components of your system, and all your software would automatically use them. The vendor of a custom display, for example, could provide a special set of "driver objects" and rest assured that all programs would use the display correctly.

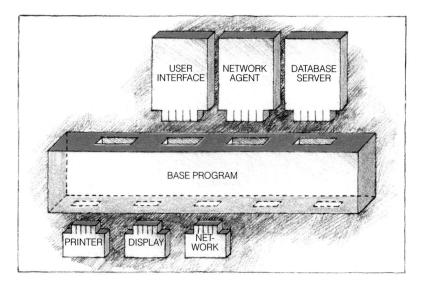

Naturally, open software is bound to create problems. No matter how
clearly the standards are defined, mismatches will always occur – user
interfaces that don't provide a required service, or programs that didn't
anticipate new display features. But open software will simplify things
as well. It's a major nuisance to have to "install" each new program, con-
figuring it to take advantage of your particular combination of hardware.
It would be a lot simpler if you could just load the appropriate interface
objects with each piece of hardware and let your programs adjust to
them automatically.

*In some cases, this
may simplify things*

Finally, open software systems would allow a lot more innovation. Most
application programs are now so complex that only established software
publishers with large programming staffs can possibly develop complete
systems. But if these systems were broken down into components that
could be mixed and matched across vendors, the small, innovative developers could get back into the fray – and that would benefit everyone.

*Open software would
promote innovation*

The Merger of Programs and Databases

Programs may merge with databases

Another change that object-oriented technology could bring about is a gradual merging of programs and databases. This may sound like a strange idea at first, but it just might prove to be a key contribution of the object-oriented movement.

Separating procedures and data violates modularity

Until recently, the division of information between programs and databases was quite strict: procedures went into programs, and data went into databases. But this division is a direct violation of modular programming, which requires that related procedures and data be packaged together. The effects of this violation are felt every time a change is made to the structure of a database. When hundreds or even thousands of programs use a shared corporate database, the consequences of even a minor change in data structures can range from a major inconvenience to a full-scale disaster.

Programs and databases

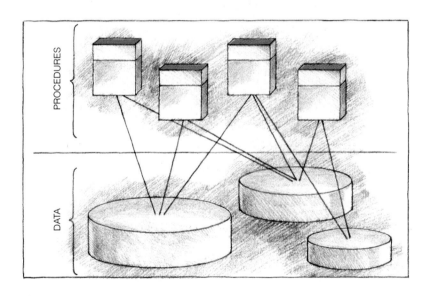

The only way to overcome this violation of modularity is to break down the distinction between programs and databases, allowing related procedures and data to be encapsulated together regardless of what applications they may serve. The active object database, which contains a complete programming language and allows methods to execute directly in the database, is the natural vehicle for bringing about this merger. The database can contain entire applications, including all their procedures as well as their data.

Procedures in object databases overcome this violation

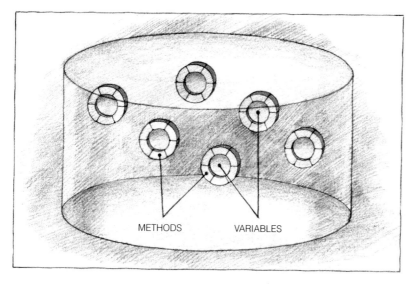

METHODS   VARIABLES

Procedures in an object database

Storing procedures in an object database yields other valuable benefits. Unlike program files, databases provide many important services such as making information available to multiple users, restricting access to qualified personnel, avoiding conflicts from concurrent access, protecting against accidental loss, and facilitating search and retrieval. When you store application procedures in an object database, they automatically benefit from all these services. In effect, the object database serves as a "procedure base" as well as a database, packaging the appropriate procedures and data together in the bargain.

There are other important benefits as well

Applications in object databases are always available

But an active object database is more than just a "procedure base," because the procedures can actually execute right in the database. The procedures are available any time they are needed, not just when some application program removes them from the database and runs them. Also, when procedures execute in the database, applications can call each other's procedures directly, using them like subroutines. Combined with the kind of mix-and-match programming described above, this arrangement results in a tremendously flexible computing environment.

This is not a return to monolithic computing

One possible objection to embedding applications in an object database is that it may imply a return to the days of monolithic computing, when all the important software ran on a central machine and was managed by a professional staff. But modern databases can be distributed over many different machines, so programmers can create and execute applications locally on their own computers. In fact, these applications could look and feel just like separate programs. The only difference is that, being constructed directly in the database, these applications could draw on the resources of all the other applications in the database.

Distributed applications in an object database

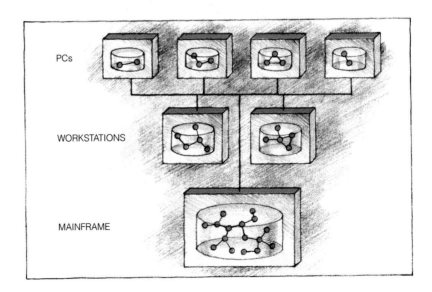

PCs

WORKSTATIONS

MAINFRAME

The advantages of embedding procedures in object databases are so great that we may see a steady migration of application programs into distributed object databases. This gradual blending of programs and data will change forever the role of the corporate database. What was once a passive repository of data will evolve into an active medium for managing not only the data but also the policies and procedures that control the operations of the company.

The corporate database will take on new importance

The Advent of Enterprise Modeling

A central tenet of the object-oriented approach is that applications should be built on top of models, with each model being used for more than one application. But if you move several applications using the same model into an object database, something interesting happens: the applications become so intertwined that they begin to lose their separate identities. In effect, the applications become no more than alternative uses of the same model. Then the focus of the computing effort shifts from developing separate applications to refining and using shared models.

Applications in object databases can merge together

This shift signals the emergence of a new kind of computing, with new goals and new techniques. Instead of constructing an on-going series of separate application programs, a company can concentrate on developing and maintaining working models of its corporate processes, enhancing those models over time to meet new needs. This model-based approach to corporate computing is called **enterprise modeling**.

This leads to a different kind of computing

An enterprise model

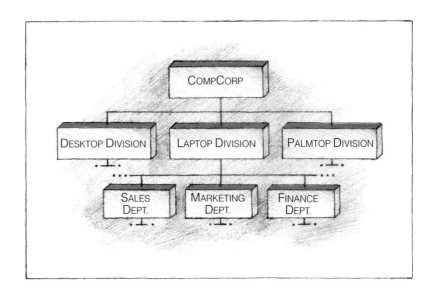

Object technology is ideal for enterprise modeling

The concept of enterprise modeling has been around for some years. What gives it new impetus today is the availability of object databases. Object-oriented technology is ideally suited to enterprise modeling because it packages corporate procedures right in with the data. And object databases provide the essential medium for distributing and sharing large-scale models.

Enterprise models provide better representations

Enterprise models can be used on several different levels. At the most basic level, they can do what databases have always done – store and retrieve information about the company. But these models can do it much better than conventional databases because they directly mirror the structure and operation of the company.

They can also be used to simulate the company

Enterprise models can also run simulations of a company's operations, allowing managers to play "what if" with their entire company. You can alter organizational structures, try out new administrative procedures or reallocate resources, and then examine the effects of these changes on your operations. Simulations such as these will allow far better planning than the simple numerical projections used by most companies today.

Finally, enterprise models can automate many procedures that are now done by hand. The document management system described in Chapter 6 is a good example of this; that system could route purchase orders, engineering diagrams, project plans, and other documents around the company for review, approval, and similar administrative procedures. Given the multimedia capabilities of object databases, there's no reason why all these documents couldn't be maintained and processed in electronic form. In short, an enterprise model running in a distributed object database could finally make the vision of a paperless office a reality.

And they can carry out corporate procedures

Summary of Key Concepts

Object-oriented technology consists of three essential mechanisms: objects, messages, and classes.

Objects

The basic unit of organization in the object-oriented approach is the object. An **object** is a software "packet" containing a collection of related data elements and a set of procedures, called **methods**, for operating on these elements. The data within an object can be accessed only by the object's methods, which handle all the routine tasks of reporting current values, storing new values, or performing calculations. This arrangement, called **encapsulation**, protects data from corruption by other objects and hides low-level implementation details from the rest of the system.

Objects combine procedures and data

Once defined, new types of objects can be used as basic data types within a program in the same way as the built-in data types that handle numbers, dates, and other elementary kinds of information. This ability to create new, high-level data structures on demand and use them in subsequent programming is called **data abstraction**. Data abstraction is central to the object-oriented approach because it allows programmers to think in terms of the problems they are solving rather than the data types of the language.

Objects provide high-level data structures

Messages

Objects communicate with one another through messages. A **message** is simply the name of a receiving object together with the name of one of its methods. A message is a request for the receiving object to carry out the indicated method and return the result of that action.

Objects communicate through messages

Any number of objects can include the same method, and each can implement it according to its own unique needs. That allows any given message to be sent to lots of different objects without worrying about how the message will be handled or even knowing what kind of object will receive it. The ability to hide implementation details behind a common message interface is known as **polymorphism**. Polymorphism makes the object-oriented approach very flexible because it allows new kinds of objects to be added to a completed system without rewriting existing procedures.

Classes

Classes describe the properties of objects

Object-oriented programming supports the repeated use of common object types through the use of classes. A **class** is a general prototype which describes the characteristics of similar objects. The objects belonging to a particular class are said to be **instances** of that class.

This is an efficient arrangement

Classes allow objects to be defined in a very efficient manner. The methods and variables for a class are defined only once, in the class definition, without repeating them in every instance of that class. The instances contain only the actual values of the variables.

Classes can inherit characteristics

Although it is possible to define classes independently of each other, classes are usually defined as special cases, or **subclasses**, of each other. Through a process called **inheritance**, all the subclasses for a given class can make use of the methods and variables of that class. Inheritance increases the efficiency of the class mechanism even further: behavior that's characteristic of larger groups of objects is programmed only once, in the definition of the higher-level class, and the subclasses merely add to or modify that behavior as required for their special cases.

Subclasses may be nested to any degree, and inheritance will accumulate down through all the levels. The resulting treelike structure is known as a **class hierarchy**. Some languages allow a class to inherit properties from more than one superclass, a feature known as **multiple inheritance**. This feature complicates matters by creating multiple overlapping hierarchies, but it permits much more flexible relationships.

Class hierarchies allow classes to be defined efficiently

Glossary

4GL

An acronym for fourth-generation language.

Abstract class

A class with no instances that's created only for the purpose of organizing a class hierarchy or defining methods and variables that will apply to lower-level classes. The term "virtual class" refers to the same concept.

Abstract data type

A data type that is defined by a programmer and not built into the programming language. Abstract data types are typically used to create high-level structures that correspond to the real-world objects represented in a program.

Bill of materials (BOM)

A term manufacturers use to describe the composition of a part or product. Each component of the product is described as a list of subcomponents. Each subcomponent is described by a list of *its* subcomponents, and so on, until the most elementary parts are identified.

C++

An object-oriented programming language developed at AT&T Bell Laboratories during the early 1980s. C++ is a "hybrid" language whose object-oriented features were grafted onto an existing language (C).

CASE

An acronym for Computer Aided Software Engineering, a collection of software tools that automate or support the process of designing and programming software systems.

Class

A template for defining the methods and variables for a particular type of object. All objects of a given class are identical in form and behavior but contain different data in their variables.

Class hierarchy

A tree structure representing the relationships among a set of classes. Class hierarchies always have one top node (which may be the *Object* class), but may have any number of levels in the tree and any number of classes at each level.

Class method

A special kind of method that's invoked by sending a message to a class rather than to one of its instances. Class methods usually perform tasks that can't or shouldn't be done at the instance level. Creating and destroying instances are examples of tasks that are usually handled by class methods.

Class variable

A special kind of variable that stores its value in the class definition rather than in the instances of that class. Class variables maintain information that's the same for all instances.

Composite object

An object that contains one or more other objects, typically by storing references to those objects in its instance variables.

Data abstraction

The process of defining new, high-level data types to serve the specialized needs of a particular application or program.

Data type

A generic description of an elementary unit of information in a particular software system. Common data types include whole numbers, decimal numbers, dollar amounts, dates, and text. Higher-level types may also be defined if abstract data types are supported.

Database management system

A program that maintains and controls access to collections of related information in electronic files. Database managers provide many services, such as regulating simultaneous access by multiple users, restricting access to authorized people, and protecting the data against damage or accidental loss.

DBMS

An acronym for a database management system.

Encapsulation

A technique in which data is packaged together with its corresponding procedures. In object-oriented technology, the mechanism for encapsulation is the object.

Enterprise modeling

The process of building and using a working model of an organization to understand the process of that organization and to implement some of its functions in software.

Expert system

A program that expresses a domain of human expertise as a set of rules, reasoning about new problems by executing those rules. Expert systems are used to identify diseases, locate mineral deposits, configure hardware systems, select stock portfolios, and perform many other useful tasks.

Fourth-generation language

A type of computer language that accepts system requirements as input and generates a program to meet those requirements as output. Fourth-generation languages, also called 4GLs, are useful primarily for well understood procedures such as the generation of menus, forms, and reports.

Functional decomposition

A technique for analyzing a set of requirements and designing a program to meet those requirements. An overall goal for the program is broken down into a series of steps to meet that goal. Each step is then decomposed into more elementary steps, and so on. Each of the resulting components is programmed as a separate module.

Hierarchic data model

A scheme for defining databases in which data elements are organized into hierarchical structures. The hierarchic model was developed in the 1960s and was the dominant type of database until the advent of the network model a decade later.

Image file

A special file used by Smalltalk to store the complete state of the system, including all current classes and objects, the image on the screen, any pending commands, and a history of past interactions.

Information hiding

The technique of making the internal details of a module inaccessible to other modules, protecting the module from outside interference, and protecting other modules from relying on details that might change over time.

Inheritance

A mechanism whereby classes can make use of the methods and variables defined in all classes above them on their branch of the class hierarchy.

Instance

A term used to refer to an object that belongs to a particular class. For example, *california* is an instance of the class *State*.

Instance method

The normal kind of method that is invoked by sending a message to an instance rather than to a class. This term is typically used to distinguish ordinary (instance) methods from the less common class methods.

Instance variable

The normal kind of variable that stores a unique value in each instance of a class. This term is typically used to distinguish ordinary (instance) variables from the less common class variables.

Message

A signal from one object to another that requests the receiving object to carry out one of its methods. A message consists of three parts: the name of the receiver, the method it is to carry out, and any parameters the method may require to fulfill its charge.

Method

A procedure contained within an object that is made available to other objects for the purpose of requesting services of that object. Most (in some languages, all) communication between objects takes place through methods.

Modular programming

A general approach to programming in which programs are broken down into components, called modules, each of which contains its own procedures and data. The central tenet of modular programming is that modules should be as independent as possible from each other, with interactions being minimized and tightly controlled.

Multiple inheritance

A scheme for structuring relationships among classes where each class can have any number of superclasses. The use of multiple inheritance permits any degree of overlap among class hierarchies, complicating the structure of the class library but providing more flexibility for defining classes.

Network data model

A scheme for defining databases in which data elements may be interconnected to any degree, forming arbitrarily complex structures. The network model was developed in the 1970s to overcome the structural limitations of the earlier hierarchic model.

Object

A software packet containing a collection of related data (in the form of variables) and methods (procedures) for operating on that data. The term is used inconsistently in the literature, referring sometimes to instances and other times to classes. In this guide, the term *object* refers to a specific instance of a class but includes the characteristics of that class. Thus, the object *AGV104* may be said to contain methods even though its methods are actually defined in the class *AutomatedVehicle*.

Object Database Management System

A database management system built specifically to store and retrieve objects rather than simple data types.

ODBMS

An acronym for an object database management system.

Object Management Group (OMG)

An industry group dedicated to promoting object-oriented technology and fostering the standardization of that technology. OMG is sponsored by member organizations, most of whom either market or develop object-oriented products.

Overloading

The assignment of multiple meanings to the same method name, allowing a single message to perform different functions depending on which object receives it and what parameters accompany it. The language automatically selects the appropriate meaning by noting the receiver and checking the number and types of the parameters.

Overriding

A special case of overloading in which the same name is given to a method or variable at two or more levels on the same branch of a class hierarchy. When this happens, the name that's lowest in the hierarchy takes precedence, overriding the more general definitions further up the hierarchy.

Paradigm

An acquired way of thinking about something that shapes thought and action in ways that are both conscious and unconscious. Paradigms are essential because they provide a culturally shared model for how to think and act, but they can present major obstacles to adopting newer, better approaches.

Paradigm shift

A transition from one paradigm to another. Paradigm shifts typically meet with considerable resistance followed by gradual acceptance as the superiority of the new paradigm becomes apparent. Object-oriented technology is regarded by many of its advocates as a paradigm shift in software development.

Parallel processing

A programming technique in which multiple activities take place at the same time. When implemented in software, the computer simulates concurrent activities by switching rapidly among tasks. When implemented in hardware, multiple processing units each take a different part of the program and process them in a truly simultaneous manner.

Parameter

A data element that's included in a message to provide the requested method with any information it may need to perform its task. A message may include any number of parameters, including zero. An alternate term for parameters is "arguments."

Polymorphism

The ability to hide different implementations behind a common interface, simplifying the communications among objects. For example, defining a unique *print* method for each kind of document in a system would allow any document to be printed by sending the message *print*, without concern for how that method was actually carried out for a given document.

Procedure

A sequence of instructions to a computer indicating how a particular task should be carried out.

Rapid prototyping

A technique of software development in which a program is developed incrementally as a series of "trial versions" that gradually converge on the desired functionality. Rapid prototyping is central to object-oriented methodology, and it differs from traditional prototyping in that an object-oriented prototype is not thrown away but refined into the deliverable system.

Receiver

The object to which a message is sent. A sender object passes a message to the receiver object, which processes the message and then passes back a return value.

Relational data model

A scheme for defining databases in which data elements are organized into relations, typically viewed as rows in tables. The relational model was developed in the 1980s to provide a more flexible alternative to the hierarchic and network models, which could not be easily restructured.

Return value

An object or data type which a receiver object passes to a sender object in response to a message.

Sender

The object initiating a message. A sender object passes a message to a receiver object and then waits for it to pass back a return value.

Simula

A computer language developed in the 1960s at the Norwegian Computing Center for the purpose of simulating real-world processes. Simula pioneered the concepts of classes, objects, and abstract data types, as well as providing object-based support for parallel processing.

Single inheritance

A scheme for structuring relationships among classes so that each class has only one superclass. Single inheritance assures that all class hierarchies will conform to a simple tree structure.

Smalltalk

An object-oriented programming language developed at Xerox PARC (Palo Alto Research Center) in the early 1970s. Smalltalk is a "pure" implementation of object-oriented concepts because it was built from the ground up to be an object-oriented system. Every entity in the system is implemented as an object.

Software crisis

A term used to describe the increasing difficulty of developing software fast enough to keep pace with business needs. The software crisis is characterized by late deliveries, cost overruns, persistent defects, and systems that are difficult to maintain and modify.

Structured programming

A collection of techniques designed to increase the rigor of software development and to improve the quality of developed systems. Modular programming and functional decomposition are central to structured programming.

Subclass

A class that is a special case of another class. For example, *Fox* is a special case of *Mammal*.

Subroutine

A sequence of instructions that has been defined as a separate unit within a program, allowing the unit to be invoked anywhere in the program simply by including its name as one of the instructions.

Superclass

A class that is higher in the class hierarchy than another class. For example, *Mammal* is a superclass of *Fox*.

Trigger

A software device that monitors the values of one or more data elements to detect critical events. A trigger consists of three components: a procedure to check the data whenever the data changes, a set or range of criterion values to determine when a response is called for, and one or more procedures that produce the appropriate response.

Variable

A storage place within an object for a data element. The data element can be a built-in data type, such as a number or a date, or it can be a reference to another object.

Virtual class

A class with no instances that's created only for the purpose of organizing a class hierarchy or defining methods and variables that will apply to all lower-level classes. The term "abstract class" refers to the same concept.

Index

About GemStone

 GemStone is the object database management system from Servio Corporation, the publishers of this book. First introduced in 1987, GemStone combines the power of object-oriented technology with the functionality and features of an industrial strength database management system.

Supporting the Object Paradigm

Readers of this book should note that GemStone supports the complete object paradigm. GemStone not only manages objects, but also manages methods. GemStone ensures consistency between stored objects and the methods that operate upon them. In addition, GemStone allows these stored methods to be executed within the database server. By supporting encapsulation within the database, GemStone goes beyond structural object servers and delivers true object data management functionality.

Flexibility for an Everchanging World

GemStone is available on a variety of hardware platforms, ranging from desktop PC and Macintosh computers, through workstations, to minicomputers. Employing an advanced client/server architecture, GemStone supports a variety of networking protocols.

GemStone protects existing investment in database and file systems by providing gateways that allow users to transparently access data stored in these systems. Applications can be programmed in many languages, including C, C++, and Smalltalk.

Notes

Notes

Notes

Notes

Notes